PICCOLO IS BLACK

A MEMOIR OF RACE, RELIGION,
AND POP CULTURE

Published by Lit Riot Press, LLC
Brooklyn, NY
www.litriotpress.com

This is a work of creative non-fiction. The events, places, and conversations in this memoir have been recreated from memory. All of the events in this memoir are true to the best of the author's memory. The names and identifying characteristics of individuals and places have been changed to maintain anonymity, some events have been compressed, and some dialogue has been recreated. The views expressed in this memoir are solely those of the author.

Book and cover design by Lit Riot Press, LLC

Library of Congress Control Number: 2021946870

Publisher's Cataloging-in-Publication Data

Name: Calhoun, Jordan.
Title: Piccolo Is Black: A Memoir of Race, Religion, and Pop Culture / Jordan Calhoun.
Identifiers: LCCN 2021946870 | ISBN 978-1-7351458-1-5 (pbk.) | ISBN 978-1-7351458-2-2 (hc.) | ISBN 978-1-7351458-3-9 (ebook).
Subjects: LCSH: Autobiographical memory. | Autobiography--African American Authors. | BISAC: BIOGRAPHY & AUTOBIOGRAPHY / Personal Memoirs. | BIOGRAPHY & AUTOBIOGRAPHY / Cultural, Ethnic & Regional / African American & Black. | BIOGRAPHY & AUTOBIOGRAPHY / General. | YOUNG ADULT NONFICTION / General. | YOUNG ADULT NONFICTION / Biography & Autobiography / General. | YOUNG ADULT NONFICTION / Biography & Autobiography / Cultural, Ethnic & Regional. | YOUNG ADULT NONFICTION / Biography & Autobiography / Literary.
Classification: LCC PS135.C15 2022 (print) DDC 810--dc23.
LC record available at https://lccn.loc.gov/2021946870.

PICCOLO IS BLACK

A MEMOIR OF RACE, RELIGION, AND POP CULTURE

JORDAN CALHOUN

LIT RIOT PRESS
BROOKLYN, NY

For Darryl

'cause see I do this for us
so dog I just write what I wanna hear

Joell Ortiz, On Da Spot Freestyle

TABLE OF CONTENTS

PREFACE   1

PART ONE   9
Praise God from Whom All Blessings Flow   11
One Shall Stand, One Shall Fall   21
Remember the Sabbath Day   31
From Sabbath to Sunday   41
The Black Fish Who Sang   53
Carry That Weight   65
Way Out Where the Dandelions Grow   75

PART TWO   83
Real Christians   85
Avalon   99
Fight Like a [Black] Girl   113
Sex Education   123
When You Believe   139
1-800-WET-GIRL   149
Tattoos and Braids   163

PART THREE   169
Healthy Choices   171
Minority Sport   181
White Power   189

Good for Nothing   201
Represent   207
Sex Education, Continued   217
Finding Miss Grotke   225

AFTERWORD   **233**

ACKNOWLEDGMENTS   **241**

ABOUT THE AUTHOR   **243**

PREFACE

I was once asked my favorite thing about my brother, Darryl. This came during a late-night texting session, the romantic phase of a new relationship where I promised one hour of complete openness for any question I was asked. I was offering to lower my defenses as a person who rarely shared what most people might consider basic insights into their lives, but it made me uncomfortable enough that I needed to set a time limit. You probably know a person like that, or met one before, the kind who redirects conversations and deflects questions from their personal life or from their past.

It was her opportunity, and after skillfully tearing down walls for several weeks in our young relationship she asked a question I hadn't expected. She passed on inquiries about ex-partners, closet skeletons, and other personal history that would have been known only to an intimate circle of friends. Instead, she asked about Darryl. She asked a seemingly throw-away question, and maybe that's how she intended it, an offering of space to show that she wouldn't push, and that I could be comfortable with less of that space when I was ready and on my own terms. And "What's your favorite thing about your brother?" was one I'd never been asked before or had even considered.

As promised, I answered, unfiltered, the first answer that came into my head. And that was when I first began to put words into this book. Aside from our shared humor and boisterous laughs, aside from loving him as my blood, my brother Darryl is the one person on earth I don't have to explain my childhood to or wonder if he understands. He was there. If I ever think I'm crazy or wonder if a certain thing happened, or if an obscure TV show existed, or a song comes up that no one else remembers, he's the proof I'm not crazy. He's the validation of my memory, my grounding to sanity.

This book wasn't meant to be a memoir. The last thing I would have wanted to write was an account of my life, the type of book that bases its value at least in part on the extent of its openness and vulnerability. I would rather you not know me, but instead know the representation of me. My name is Jordan, I'm a writer in Harlem, New York, home of James Baldwin, Zora Neale Hurston, and Langston Hughes. I'm a returned Peace Corps volunteer. I studied three languages. I hold a B.A. in Sociology and Criminal Justice, a B.S. in Psychology with a minor in Japanese, and an M.P.A. in Public and Nonprofit Management and Policy. I love nerd culture and I learned long ago that unabashed confidence in being a nerd is key to navigating professional adulthood without being seen as unusual in the wrong way.

What this book *was* intended to be was a collection of essays about the TV and movies I loved as a child. But as I wrote about each one of them, there was a trend in their functions, so often that I began to feel I was writing the same thing over and over. I cared less about what happened behind the scenes of my favorite stories and more about what they meant to me at that stage in my life. I didn't care about the publisher, studio, or producer. I didn't care about the actors, or how the sausage was made. There was only the story, and what those characters meant for me as I came to define who I was and would become.

I planned to discuss TV and movies without any context of why they were meaningful to me. There was that option, and plenty of other, better writers have paved the way by writing books and essays, with research and inside information on the history that allowed writers, actors, producers, animators, engineers, directors, studios, and investors to make the things I loved. I planned to write without the discomfort of sharing the parts of myself I found embarrassing.

What I hope you find in the coming chapters is that I chose discomfort. I chose to share my niche little thoughts so that in some way I could honor those writers, actors, producers, animators, engineers, directors, studios, and investors for what they created. To thank them for what they did for me, whether or not they knew or even intended what they were doing for me.

If you grew up around the 1980s and '90s, you might have a shared cache of pop culture experiences, such as memories of collecting Pogs and raising Gigapets, magazine tear-outs of musicians on walls, an opinion on Backstreet Boys versus N'Sync, Tupac versus Biggie, or Britney versus Christina, board game and action figure commercials, or the inability to get the Mr. Bucket song out of your head whenever the name Mr. Bucket was mentioned. There were Saturday morning cartoons and TGIF, the cereals you wanted and the ones your parents let you eat. You maybe share in the unwavering assurance that our collective childhood held the best of everything in entertainment, such as the Golden Age of Disney, the arms race of video game development, and music videos on *TRL* and *106 & Park*.

Much of the television, movies, music, and books we loved was dependent on Black culture without crediting it, while others excluded the non-white experience altogether, leaving Black consumers to adapt to it by either learning to ignore our absence, or loving what wasn't made with us in mind. I chose the latter, as I think many of us did. And for those of us who did and continue to ride along in the adventure of the Black experience in pop culture, it's quite the rollercoaster.

That's what this story is all about. It's about growing up Black, navigating cultures, learning what was and wasn't intended for me, that often I was not the default audience but would still find myself in the mix of it all, loving and learning the mental gymnastics needed to find myself in characters where it wasn't so clear, refining my empathy until I could see anything and make it my own. How I unknowingly navigated by making attachments, both obvious and unspoken, to characters and themes to relate to the cultures around us.

Having something "for you" is powerful. Having something "meant for you" is special. It's a treasure to cherish and hold to your chest for people of color, women, LGBTQ people, people with disabilities, for anyone outside of what popular media and marketing executives would consider their standard audience, the people they traditionally served.

For those who have ever felt left out, our journeys may have been different, but where the terrain is the same, I hope we find value, whether through a flood of nostalgia, insight into entertainment once considered frivolous or unworthy of thought, or a laugh. Or all the above.

This is also for me. This story is told in the hope that many of us felt the same, and that the more personal we get, the more relatable we reveal ourselves to be. It follows then that just a representation of me wouldn't do. I would have to step out of the dressing room clothed in my weird little life in hopes that you accept those clothes, or better yet, you like them because your life is a closet of weird clothes too, or even better yet, though we wear them differently many of the colors are the same, and a few patterns are the same, and holy shit, look at us, maybe we can both walk outside dressed like this.

So, my name is Jordan, I'm a writer in Harlem, New York, but I haven't finished *Go Tell It on the Mountain* or *Their Eyes Were Watching God*, and I grew up in so many neighborhoods, cities, and suburbs that I feel I'm from nowhere at all. I'm a returned Peace Corps volunteer where I ran a few programs I'm proud of, where I mostly staved off depression in a small Eastern European city. I speak three foreign languages but never got past intermediate proficiency in any of them, and I speak them poorly enough now that I should probably stop saying that I speak them at all. I hold a B.A. in Sociology and Criminal Justice, a B.S. in Psychology with a minor in Japanese, and an M.P.A. in Public and Nonprofit Management and Policy. All this education meant that I took on $115,000 in student debt on the promise that education was my way out the hood, and that if I had enough of it then white people might finally look at me differently than the way I saw them looking at me. I love nerd culture, and I learned long ago that unabashed confidence in being a nerd is key to distracting others from my worse insecurities.

This book is a cathartic purge of everything I learned, obsessed over, sang, argued, and memorized as a part of what should be the most wonderful time in life. It's about me growing up and about the things that raised me.

One of those things is TV, for better or worse. Movies,

cartoons, video games, and comics met me at my level by speaking to me in a way that I would listen. They affected my life more than most teachers. They still affect me today. It's a secret that non-nerds are only just beginning to uncover, that those mediums still meet us at our level now. Non-nerds were tricked into believing something like anime was only for kids, while the rest of us kept on until now, when being well-read also means having read your share of books made of pictures and voice bubbles. Each summer blockbuster season carries the influence of a story adapted from anime, graphic novels, or reboots of an old cartoon, and tomorrow's movies will be recognized by nerds as further adaptations of indie comics and other stories being written, drawn, and animated today. In a way, turning "nerd" pastimes into mainstream interests is the fulfillment of the prophesies I saw as a child, cliché as they were, that nerds would persevere in the end.

What a time to be alive, and what a time to have lived, to have grown from a child to an adult. And now that I'm here, with the emotional distance that adulthood brings, my next stage of learning is an equally important one.

In writing this book, I hoped to understand the joy of what entertained me, the lessons that my childhood taught, and the traumas and triumphs of the boy I was. I hoped to look back through the rose-colored lens of nostalgia to remember who I was and what I loved, but also be brave enough to take the glasses off to see those experiences more truthfully. Some of them are ugly, in hindsight. Some are embarrassing. Many of them are sad. But along the way, I hoped to recapture the feeling of loving something in a way that only a 12-year-old could, with every ounce of unfettered excitement. The moments where nothing else existed, because that thing meant the world to me. I like to think those moments are so pure that if I can hold onto even a fraction of their undiluted form, then the Toys "R" Us song would be proven right, that I didn't have to grow up, not all the way.

These are love letters to nerd culture. They are love letters to Black people. They are love letters to Black nerd culture, the intersection where I lived, that helped me survive in the same way you might have learned to survive, by finding something, anything, to use as a mirror to reflect a version of yourself that could only survive. This is a homage to 12-year-old me, to my friends, and to my brother Darryl. Diversity in media in the '80s, '90s, and '00s is all disconnected dots, and if the way to connect them was for me to write a memoir, then I guess I had to write a memoir. This is my childhood, my discomfort with it, my celebration of it. It's the pop culture that helped form my identity. Like Bane in the *The Dark Knight Rises*, I was born in it. Molded by it.

To the extent you can relate I thank you, because that's the reason I began to write this book, to know that while some of it may feel embarrassing, our experiences are not uncommon. To know that someone saw what I saw, remembers what I remember, and to know that it was important to them too. To those who sang "Father Abraham" and "Zacchaeus Was a Wee Little Man" on weekends and later struggled to find peace with their church, and to those who knew Piccolo was Black from the moment they saw him. This book is a celebration of our adaptation through white supremacist pop culture, our survival through religious zealotry, and our navigation through psychologically treacherous minefields. Come celebrate with me. You're family, too.

PART ONE

"When I was a child, I spoke as a child, I
understood as a child, I thought as a child; but
when I became a man, I put away childish things."
- 1 Corinthians 13:11

"Remember who you are." - Mufasa

CHAPTER 1

PRAISE GOD FROM WHOM ALL BLESSINGS FLOW

"This wasn't made for you." My grandma reached to take the patch from my hand, my hard-earned reward for having studied tents and ropes for weeks, memorizing their loops and ties until my fingers could make a fisherman's knot off muscle memory. Granted, at nine years old I had never fished, and I had gone camping maybe once by then, yet the patch represented my weeks of work, so I didn't care if my newfound skill was ever needed. Since when did "need" matter, anyway? I had one more patch to add to my sash for Pathfinders, the Seventh-day Adventist analog to the Boy and Girl Scouts.

"Hand it to me," my grandma said in her Jamaican accent, pointing to one patch in particular, and so I did, and she brought it close to her eyes as I wondered why she was taking it away. On the patch knelt two kids made of needle and thread, building a campsite. I'd earned my share of patches that year, learning to tie knots and pitch tents, identify flowers and recite proper fire safety rules. My proudest patch came from a masterful knowledge of wild cats, an obsession I had that led me to checkout out every book from the library on jaguars, leopards, and panthers.

"What's the scientific name for cats?" my Pathfinder leader had asked me, indignant of my wanting to test for the patch without taking the required courses.

"*Felix*," I said. I knew from Felix the Cat, the first animated cartoon to ever be monetized and one of the most the most recognized cartoon characters of its century. A moment of surprise flashed across his face and was quickly hidden, but not before I had a hunch that first, he might've thought it was a hard question, and second, that I genuinely knew more than he expected. "And the name for big cats is *panthera felix*," I added, my nine-year-old confidence so far from Earth that I needed to get ahead of his questions to break his spirit, and to keep him from even trying to stump me. "Come on, challenge me," I said to an adult, the earliest trash-talk of my entire life coming from knowing everything there was to know about big, wild cats at nine years old.

Months later, after my Pathfinder leader gave me my worksheet to earn my cats badge, I learned to tie knots and pitch tents, something that didn't come naturally, and so I was proud of this new patch I had earned even if knots weren't nearly as interesting as murderous cats. "I'll give it back," my grandma told me, and I thought to whine, but it was clear that I wasn't being punished, that she knew some secret, like the threads were fatally frayed in a place only grandmas could see, and she needed to repair it before it all fell apart. *This wasn't made for you*, though.

Old people speak in riddles, so I dismissed the thought behind basketball and toys, up until a few hours later after I'd completely forgotten the patch even existed. She called me from across the hall and into her room. "Here's your patch, Jordan. You can take it back," and she gestured to the dresser where it sat, and then went back to watching her TV.

Sweet, I'll add it to my sash, I thought as I picked it up and looked at it. Of the two kids on the patch knelt in front of the campsite, sewn of light pink thread, she'd undone one of them, and resewed him in brown thread. I looked over at grandma, but she was enthralled in her game show, no longer paying attention, satisfied with having done this small thing, this important thing she needed to do, like now she could casually go back to her day. And I ran back to play with my toys.

I grew up at 19474 Sorrento, on the west side of Detroit, Michigan. It was a colonial-style house in the middle of the block, central enough to be the 50-yard line in street football, but far enough from the main intersection to be safe. The house belonged to my grandma, who purchased it after leaving Jamaica for the United States with my mother in 1963.

My mom, brother, and I moved into my grandma's house after my parents' divorce when I was around six, leaving our small bungalow house at 17164 Braille that I barely recall but for a few memories, like pouring orange juice in my oatmeal, putting together my first bike, being chased by a dog, or being forced to sit at the table until I finished that god-awful oatmeal. I saw my father on weekends at 19014 Revere Street, on the east side of the city.

Later, when my mom was ready to move back out on her own, we would leave grandma's house for the Detroit northern suburb of Southfield. There we would live at 9 Mile Road in a townhouse complex called Roanoke Place, then on to 6841 Rutland, occasionally staying with my dad at 11645 Stahelin. Eventually I would leave Detroit to attend college in Kalamazoo in western Michigan, where I lived at 722 Wheaton, then

1300 Concord Place, and finally 755 Dragonfly.

Altogether, I have lived in more than 20 places across five countries from my childhood to my current home in New York City, so the question of where I'm from can feel challenging. It sometimes was difficult to answer that question from other Black people where the question carries its unique cultural weight, but I had much more trouble answering it to another population I would come to know well after I was pulled from school in Detroit at 13 years old and transplanted to suburban Michigan. That population was white Americans.

When a white person asks where I'm from, at least a part of their motivation tends to feel like they are sizing up my background against the person standing in front of them. Are you from the suburbs, or did you come from the city? Questions that lend themselves to "you speak so well," the proverbial pat on the head after a white person asks, "*Detroit*-Detroit?" As if to ask, what kind of Black are you?

I would spend years learning to answer that question for others, to offer an explanation that clarified the person they saw in front of them. I would feel like the Monet effect personified. From a distance I was a painting that made sense, but the closer you looked, the more confusing it became.

The Detroit I knew was split in half, both literally and figuratively. In the literal sense, Detroit was the east side and the west side. For me, though, it was Seventh-day Adventists against the world that lived in sin and didn't follow the Sabbath.

Five days a week, from elementary school through junior high, I attended Detroit Urban Lutheran School, a medium-sized, all-Black school that was little different from a public school except that being technically private meant that teachers could hit students. I would keep track of the number of times I was paddled per year, and by which teachers. My first year there I was paddled eight times by Ms. Nelson, a no-nonsense teacher most memorable for being feared and for the large mole on her nose, a real-life Ms. Swamp from the *Miss Nelson Is Missing!* cassette I had played on repeat.

Our most notable alumnus was NFL Hall of Famer Jerome Bettis, who was also spanked by Ms. Nelson, a connection that made him my favorite NFL running back. Twice in second grade, when she was my homeroom teacher, she got fed up enough to paddle the entire class, so that counted for two of the eight paddles that year. Another time, I had asked the Teacher's Assistant if I could go to the bathroom, and she said yes, but Andre Barksdale tackled me on the way out the door because he wanted to leave the classroom first. It was just then that Ms. Nelson walked in, saw us on the ground, and paddled us both.

I was a casualty of those three paddles, but the other five times were likely deserved, at least to the extent an elementary school-aged student could deserve to be paddled by their teachers. In third grade I was paddled by Ms. Prue, and in fourth grade by Mrs. Henry, two white women with weak arms and fiberglass paddles. The fiberglass paddles were shaped like the wooden ones, but were thinner with holes for aerodynamics, and the rumor was that they hurt more than the regular, 2-inch-thick wood paddle. I learned that was more myth than reality.

In fifth grade I was paddled by Mr. Hughes five times, and those were the closest I came to crying, which I'd taken pride in avoiding. He used the wooden paddle, and his technique was impeccable, looping a finger into your back belt loop and pulling up as high and he could to make clean contact with your ass through your jeans.

In sixth grade, Ms. Winston made it a rule that if any her homeroom students got paddled by another teacher, they'd get a paddle from her as well, so my count automatically doubled. My best friends got paddled with me, Jason Brooks, Allen Jennings, Xavier Henry, and Terrell Hicks. We got paddled for all manners of transgressions that we hid from our parents, lest they find out and want to spank us too. It was the '90s, and while most places had moved on from corporal punishment for children, Detroit lagged behind.

On Saturdays though, I attended either Detroit Center Seventh-day Adventist Church or Northwest Seventh-day Adventist Church, depending on which parent had custody that weekend. Both were medium-sized, all-Black churches that felt little different from most protestant churches except that we went to church on Saturdays. There too I could be spanked by other adults for stepping out of line, but it was also where I learned a fear stronger than physical punishment. That fear was that God was omniscient, omnipotent, and omnipresent, and his son Jesus died for my sins such that any time I sinned, either in deed or in my heart, it retroactively counted toward the pain he felt when he bore my burden on a hill called Calvary.

In between Detroit Urban Lutheran School and the two Adventist churches, I lived on the streets where I saw the city in the spaces between my two bubbles. I knew the city in absolute terms, which is to say I understood everything about my life in Detroit without knowing what it meant relative to anything else.

I knew that we were poor, which was a simple fact of life, because I just didn't know anyone rich.

I knew that we were Black, which was also a simple fact of life, because I didn't know anyone who wasn't Black aside from the Arab families who befriended my mom and clerked the corner stores that I would browse for Flamin' Hot Cheetos, Faygo, Better Made chips, and 2-for-$1 honey buns.

I knew to fear the drug dealers on the corner, which was again a simple fact of life, as any encounter with them could mean a threat to my body.

Another simple fact of life was that I knew if someone gave me the ultimatum between my shoes and my life, I should give them my shoes, if only I had expensive enough shoes to solicit such an ultimatum.

I knew that if a dealership came to repossess your car, you could fight the repo man, or threaten to fight them, and since they couldn't take your car away by force, you had to keep watch and know when to hop out, or otherwise keep your car parked in different places.

I knew that if everyone was running away from something, or if my older brother, Darryl, said to run, that I should run without hesitation or question, in the direction everyone else was running.

The only nuance I understood that separated me from those around me was that I was of God's chosen church, instilled with a sense of sin, knowledge, and responsibility to "be in the world but not of the world," as the Bible told us. It was that sense of virtue that sometimes spilled over to Detroit Urban Lutheran School where I would win a large trophy for the Christian Life Award at the end of a school year, but that I would otherwise keep siloed from my street-kid friends who let me be a street kid along with them. In church it was "praise God from whom all blessings flow," and at school it was playing thumps until your knuckles were sore. In church it was "bring all the tithes into the storehouse," and at school it was losing a bag of peanut M&Ms on a game of spades at the lunch table. In church it was "oh, we are the Pathfinders strong" and "soon and very soon we are going to see the king," and at school it was discussing the lyrics of Adina Howard's "Freak Like Me" as if we understood what any of the lyrics meant.

My weeks were a seesaw between my non-Adventist days and my Adventist nights and weekends, two circles of my life's Venn diagram that had little overlap. The only people who understood the delicate steps across the two worlds were other Adventist kids, like my older brother Darryl, but even among the dual-culture Adventist kids, most had chosen to prioritize one side or the other. Adventist kids who chose Christ, or whose families were attentive enough to effectively choose for them, attended Seventh-day Adventist schools. Some, like one family from Detroit Center SDA Church, guarded their television closely enough that their kids automatically muted commercial breaks when I hung out with them, because commercials couldn't be properly vetted in advance by their parents. Some kids couldn't watch TV at all and just accepted it.

Those who prioritized the non-Adventist world attended church just as regularly, or even more than others, by being forced into Pathfinders weekday youth programs like Adventist Youth, or A.Y. for short, and into adult prayers meetings by parents who aimed to keep them off the streets, hoping that the church's many activities would plant a seed of righteousness that would be sunned and watered until their children reconsidered their priorities.

Where most kids seemingly chose a side though, my brother and I were in the minority of Adventist kids who managed to walk the line, to straddle both the Adventist and non-Adventist world by having divorced parents who were involved enough to bring us to church, but tired or inattentive enough to give us some distance to just be kids. We had the rules of an Adventist home with none of the enforcement, meaning that while we weren't allowed to celebrate a Satanic holiday like Halloween, or read demonic books like *Goosebumps*, or watch cartoons that celebrate the occult like *Pokémon*, we most certainly could without much effort when we wanted. And we wanted often.

This freedom allowed Darryl and me to be fluent in both cultures, to be one version of ourselves with our non-Adventist friends and another version when we stepped foot in the church or were around other Adventists. There was a social contract to keep the worlds separate to allow us to thrive in both. And it worked 99 percent of the time, except for the occasional event when our mom would mention the Sabbath as an explanation for why we couldn't attend a weekend school activity, or when a more pious Adventist kid breached the contract by discussing our faith in mixed company.

Their penchant for dry snitching about our faith in mixed company was partially why dual-culture Adventist kids like my brother and I made closer friends with the less-pious kids from church, the ones more street kid than the Christian kids, the ones of whom adults were wary and quietly judged under the guise of sending extra prayers their way. Antoine Jackson and Deshawn Williams were two of those kids, and both became best friends with Darryl, and being the younger tagalong brother that I was, I considered them my friends, too. Our vocabulary was a mix of Adventist vocabulary and hood talk, mentioning "Sister Johnson" or "Brother Calhoun" one minute and who got robbed the next.

And that was my Detroit. Poor, Black, pious, and beautiful. I felt beautiful when non-Adventist parents would dote about how well I behaved, because an Adventist kid who was also paddled in school knew how to behave when he wanted. I felt part of a community when a parent would pick up their kids from school and, when seeing me begin my mile-long walk home, would tell me to get in because they knew where I lived, and nobody walked in a city built for driving. I felt brilliant when we played my favorite trivia game at A.Y. on Thursday evenings at church, where each kid stood next to a church pew and could move forward one pew for each question they got right, and I saw the physical representation of my being ahead, a living game board piece on his way to being first to the altar.

All I was really missing was to feel chosen here on earth, to feel part of a family after my parents had broken up, so I resolved as a kid to get them back together in a child-like, hopeful way that was inspired by a VHS tape that my grandma owned of the 1961 film *The Parent Trap*. Both Darryl and I watched it on repeat, though I suspected he didn't know how serious the goal was to be taken. As far as I was concerned, *The Parent Trap* was instructional, and we would have to come up with our own ways to compensate for the fact that we weren't twins who were separated by our parents, and that we couldn't switch places in order to reunite them.

CHAPTER 2

ONE SHALL STAND, ONE SHALL FALL

If *The Parent Trap* was work and church was a moral responsibility, cartoons were freedom. I was 11 years old in 1996 when *Beast Wars* premiered, bringing computer animation to the small screen following the success of Disney's first computer-animated film produced by a little-known studio named Pixar. That film was 1995's *Toy Story*, and with *Beast Wars* I was able to see computer-made graphics each weekday as the Maximals fought the Predacons in a quest to return home.

Different from previous iterations of the franchise, *Beast Wars* took place on a planet without humans and served as a type of prequel to the more familiar *The Transformers: The Movie*. Megatron and the Decepticons had been on a mission for energon, the power source that keeps Transformers alive, when Optimus Prime and the Autobots were sent to stop them from gaining the advantage in their war. When their space battle resulted in a transwarp device tearing through the space-time continuum, both the Decepticons and their Autobot pursuers found themselves on a prehistoric planet. To survive, they scanned the planet for native lifeforms and transformed into them to adapt to the new land, and *Beast Wars* was born.

Optimus Prime became Optimus Primal, a gorilla instead of his traditional semi-truck, Megatron became a tyranno-saurus rex, and true to the character's pride and arrogance, kept his name. Autobots became known as Maximals and were based mostly on mammals, while Decepticons became Predacons and were based mostly on reptiles and insects.

I had entered a Transformers phase from watching the animated *Transformers: The Movie*, which turned into an obsession. My brother had "borrowed" the VHS from one of his friends in that way one "borrows" things in Elementary school with the assumption that you can loan that thing to others. That's how your video games ended up down the street at your friend's neighbor's cousin's house, and how my brother handed *Transformers: The Movie* to me.

It was a fitting change of possession though, because no one could have loved that VHS more than me. In my daily ritual, I jumped off the bus from school after arguing about the latest from *Mighty Morphin Power Rangers* or *Pokémon*, walked in the house through the side door, through the kitchen, and to the den where I tossed my bag on the couch and pressed play as I quoted the opening words to the movie all alone. I was content in my being a more carefree Black boy than I ever have been and ever will be.

The first words of the 1986 animated movie *Transform-ers* are "It is the year 2005," telling the now familiar story of the alien race of advanced technology. From *Transformers* to *Back to the Future* to *The Jetsons*, I imagined a world looking entirely different even in the near future, complete with hover boards, holograms, and flying cars. It was the opposite of my weekend imagination of a near future that I was taught would bring "troubled times," and I sequestered the opposing beliefs to their respective worlds. In one, the future was an epic fantasy. In the other, the world was destined to fall into wickedness, desolation, and plagues until the Last Days and the return of Jesus Christ came to save me.

I sat captivated by the TV, re-watching each scene as if for the first time. The earliest shock came in what was a mere introduction to the Decepticons, where I sat unblinking as the they hijacked a ship, shot lasers at unsuspecting Autobots who rallied, returned fire, and…wait, did they die? Are they dead? All of them? It couldn't be right. And just like that, *Transformers* was my earliest example of a cartoon where death was real, a thing that could actually happen in the same way I was told it could happen, just outside when you were outnumbered or too weak or couldn't pedal your bike fast enough to get away. They were throwaway characters in the way I would be a throwaway character to a stranger who decided my role in their movie would be a minor one.

I didn't want to be minor. I wanted to matter, and I sat in that feeling as I met Hot Rod and Danny, the other end of the spectrum from the Decepticons' terror.

"If you're gonna ride, Danno," Hot Rod said to Danny as they ran side by side, Hot Rod in his anthropomorphic form before jumping in towards the sky and transforming mid-air to catch Danny in his driver's seat, "Ride in style."

That moment of absolute inconsequence was anything but inconsequential to a boy who wanted to be special. What I would have given to run and transform in the air, or as a consolation prize, to have a friend who could transform and catch me in his driver's seat as we sped towards adventure. Having a place to run would even be enough, the need to run, because something is urgent, because something or someone needs you.

And off they ran in service to the greatest leader of all, the one and only Optimus Prime, carrier of the matrix of leadership, the orb that signified his position. The matrix had another purpose, though, which was to open and release its power in the world's darkest hour so that good could triumph over evil.

As it turned out, the matrix was sort of an ass. If you had answered the call to protect the world and were named leader of that cause, you might assume the matrix would respect you enough to save your metal skin if your life were in danger. It would behoove the world you were protecting if you stayed alive, you would think. Except you would be wrong, as I learned anew every weekday on the couch after school when Optimus Prime fought Megatron.

Optimus Prime versus Megatron began with the noble words of the world's most noble warrior, "Megatron must be stopped…no matter the cost." Good must prevail over evil. The Autobots must win. This is why he led, why the matrix chose him. Cue the most inspirational song that I still sing in my heart when I need strength, despite never telling anyone, because who could ever understand, except everyone who has ever felt their soul rise to the guitar riff of "The Touch," an '80s power ballad by rock singer Stan Bush? With the guitar screaming in the background, Optimus transforms into a truck on his way towards danger, and I cannot say this hyped enough, literally drives through two Decepticons. One leaps out of the way while three others begin firing on Prime, who then drops his cargo box, transforms into the air back into his robot form, and blasts each of them with a cannon so big it needs both his hands to carry.

And then he sees him. They see each other. Optimus Prime stands opposite Megatron, and Optimus says the words of nerd legend, the words that told me this is really it. There will be no parley, no negotiations. We won't run to fight another day. We won't have this same fight ever again. This is game seven.

"One shall stand, one shall fall."

And it was Optimus who fell. Optimus Prime, leader of the Autobots and carrier of the matrix of leadership.

But not before he wrecked Megatron so bad that he nearly died, too. Their fight was levels above what I had seen from arrogant heroes against outmatched villains, or falsely confident villains against reluctant heroes. Megatron said "I'll kill you with my bare hands" and Prime said "bring it." Optimus and Megatron crashed to the floor in a whirl of electricity that surrounded them. Seeing the boss is in trouble, Hot Rod wanted to come through screaming "Regulators" with the extra horses and the burners like Chavez in *Young Guns*, but Cup told him to fall back because it's on Prime to do or die. Hot Rod would just get in the way and get him killed.

Optimus had it covered anyway, though, as Megatron was hurled backward into a dilapidated wall behind him, and you just knew O.G. Prime was about to rush his ass against the ropes. The shoeshine was coming, the bicycle kick, maybe a shoulder rush straight to the sternum. Optimus geared up to rush, but he took too long. He stood like a deer in headlights as Megatron picked up a spear of debris, sharp as a stake, and turned into the first Cy Young-winning Decepticon. That spear hurdled through your hopes, your dreams, your fears and aspirations. By the time you blinked Optimus had a foreign object making friends with his digital organs.

Optimus pulled the joint out from his waist and his ConEdison meter started going down. Megatron's internal dialogue yelled "he's cut!" like Duke Evers in *Rocky IV* and he blasted the cannon, but Prime slipped the shot, and just like that began a new round.

Megatron rifled through his weapons inventory, cannon, pistol, battle debris, here it is, and he pulled out a light saber to slash Prime in the exact same spot because he knew those ribs were tender. Megatron was doing targeted advertising on Prime's right side that was already leaking battery acid and energon, and Prime was holding his side trying to keep his toy parts in, slowly backing towards a death pit that was behind him. Megatron saw the end as he leapt ten feet in the air, light saber above his head, swinging down for the death blow with the sun shining behind him. And then Optimus showed us why he's a real G, the one the matrix had chosen. Prime hit down, diagonal, forward, and connected with Megatron's jaw with the rising dragon punch. It was officially a dog fight.

They grappled, arms tangled in arms, hands digging into each other's faces, and Prime took his advantage. With the plant of his left foot, a hip to the body, and an arm in his hand, Optimus judo threw Megatron, and that was it. Prime had finally won. He had bested Megatron head to head, hand to hand, toe to toe.

"Finish him off, Prime!" yelled an onlooking Cup, having had faith in his leader all along as Prime walked calmly to the gun that lay on the ground, ready to give Megatron the long kiss goodnight.

"No more, Optimus Prime! Grant me mercy, I beg you!" Megatron said.

Megatron…pleading? Submissive? And that's when we

learned something about the leader of the Decepticons. That's when I saw in him what I hoped to find in bullies, a buried fear, one that rises when you add heat.

Except Megatron was reaching for a gun just outside of Prime's sight.

Noticing the gun, Hot Rod sprang onto the scene to rescue his leader and tried to pull the gun from Megatron's hand. Prime yelled for Hot Rod to get out of the way, but it was too late. Megatron grabbed Hot Rod and took him hostage, blocking Optimus from having a clear shot. And Megatron shot Prime in his side.

The same side. He fired a second time. And a third.

"Fall, Prime! Fall!" Megatron yelled.

And on the fourth shot, Prime did fall.

"One shall stand, one shall fall," and it was Optimus who fell. Optimus Prime, leader of the Autobots and carrier of the matrix.

Gun pointed, Megatron looked down at his fallen enemy.

"It's over, Prime." And with his last ounce of strength, with every drop of energon left in his body, Optimus Prime said "Never."

I needed a minute. This was a whole different movie.

Decades after my afternoons on the couch, just me, my backpack, and a worn VHS, I met the creator of the Transformers, Bob Budiansky, although "creator" is a loose definition, of sorts. Transformers had existed before Budiansky in the form of toys manufactured by an American company named Hasbro, the same company behind half the toys that were in my toy box, including G.I. Joe, Nerf, Stretch Armstrong, Trolls, Popples, and Pound Puppies. Transformers as I knew them were the result of Hasbro wanting to raise the popularity of their characterless toys by giving them names and personalities, and it was Bob Budiansky's job to do just that, name them, add personalities, and give them a purpose.

He made Starscream jealous, and he made Grimlock into what could be described as Homer Simpson meets Cookie Monster. He drafted personality traits for Autobots and Decepticons one by one, drafting names he felt fit with their structure and personality. Soundwave. Devastator. Ultra Magnus. Hasbro gave him the creative flexibility to bring life to their lifeless figures and invent them as we know them today.

But occasionally they pushed him to try something different. Bosses at Hasbro would ask Budiansky to change details here or there so they could better sell toys, and he largely complied with their requests. They were a paycheck, after all, and it was a good gig from a popular employer worth keeping happy. Only once did he push back.

In the wake of nuclear terror in the early 1980s from the United States and the Soviet Union, Hasbro sent Bob Budiansky one name back, telling him to change it. The name was too menacing sounding, they said. The character was too powerful, too nuclear, too evil. That name was "Megatron."

To Bob though, Megatron couldn't be "too evil." This was the Lord of Darkness, the villain who wanted to rule and destroy. Menacing? Evil? That's how he was supposed to sound. And for the first time Budiansky pushed back, standing by the villain he created. The villain who wanted to rule, who stood against Optimus Prime.

To think, we were one decision away losing that guy. One acquiescence away from losing "Fall, Prime! Fall!" and "It's over, Prime," and "Never." No one knows who that Megatron would have been, but I'd take my chances with this one over any alternate universe I could imagine. This Megatron and this Optimus Prime. These Autobots and these Decepticons. Those school day afternoons, through the kitchen and to the den where I tossed my bag on the couch and watched "It is the year 2005" all alone, a more carefree Black boy than I ever had been and ever would be.

Darryl and I would meet our own Megatron just a few years later, though I wouldn't know it at the time. I'd just be a little boy who wanted a place to run towards, who wanted to matter, who loved adventure. At 11 years old, watching those adventures teleported me from the weekend's spiritual battles between good and evil into a world where I could sit detached from the Biblical war, invulnerable to its sin and its salvation, its heaven and its hell.

CHAPTER 3

REMEMBER THE SABBATH DAY

I figured out early that being Christian was considered normal, but being Seventh-day Adventist was considered weird. Or, at least, it felt strange enough to be worth hiding from kids at school. Darryl's silence on the topic at school was an unspoken agreement to what I already knew, that we weren't Catholic, Baptist, Lutheran, or Episcopalian, but we were Seventh-day Adventist, and that was weird.

I learned that my church was a chosen church of a chosen people. I was to study the Bible closer than others and honor the proper Sabbath. I was to invite you to church on the Sabbath and be prepared to challenge your understanding of the Bible. I wouldn't join the Boy Scouts, but the Pathfinders. I wouldn't attend a public university, but Andrews or Loma Linda. I would follow the teachings of the prophet Ellen G. White, a woman chosen by God to lead his people. Most importantly, every Sabbath, I would go into God's sanctuary on His holy day and worship.

The fourth commandment was the strongest pillar of my family's faith and was the longest of God's commands passed down to Moses on Mount Sinai, weighing in just shy of 100 words. I was taught that it was also the forgotten commandment because other Christians would disregard the sanctity of the Sabbath. This would be their cause for damnation and the source of a unique Adventist pride, having been proudly raised in God's truth to know better.

Sometimes during food drives and other charity events I would notice our adults witnessing to others, and I could tell that strangers were, at best, only passingly familiar with our faith. We believed in the Sabbath, that Saturday is a holy day to be kept sacred as a day of rest, worship, and reflection. Our belief in the Sabbath was based on the fourth commandment, which I had learned by heart as early as I can remember. I would repeat the commandment with our church congregation, a collective pronouncement of the foundation on which our church stands:

Remember the Sabbath day to keep it holy. Six days shall thou labor and do all thy work, but the seventh day is the Sabbath of the Lord thy God. In it, thou shalt not do any work. Thou, nor thy sons, nor thy daughters, nor thy manservant, nor thy maidservant, nor thy shepherd, nor thy stranger that is within thine gates. For in six days the Lord made heaven and Earth, the sea, and all that in them is, and rested the seventh day, wherefore the Lord blessed the seventh day, and hallowed it.

Specific rules around the Sabbath varied depending on families and regions, from simply taking the day off work, to a more conservative view that included preparing your food the day beforehand because cooking on the Sabbath would be work itself. In Michigan, my family was closer to the latter.

During the Sabbath, prayer, hymns, and Bible-study were encouraged. I couldn't watch TV, play sports or video games, cook, clean, or listen to secular music. As a general rule, if I had to question whether it brought glory to God, it likely didn't and shouldn't be done on that Sabbath. Among the most cherished values I learned from Adventism was the value of sacrifice, as the stricter I was in my beliefs, and the more I sacrificed, the holier I was meant to feel.

Still, different households kept different standards that led to philosophical Seventh-day Adventist discussions. I was aware of the cooking debate, where some families would chop, mix, and otherwise prepare the food for the Sabbath on Friday before sunset so they could easily pop it in the oven on Saturday. Others would fully cook the food on Friday and simply warm it in the oven on Sabbath, as reheating was considered a better option than full-blown cooking. Others abstained from oven use altogether, leaning towards the efficiency of a microwave. Another debate I considered with the childhood mindset of a devout Adventist was swimming versus wading, where some would consider swimming on the Sabbath to be sinful, while others argued the utility of exercise for maintaining health. Of course, I just wanted to play, and I would occasionally test the losing argument that basketball made me happy and thus had spiritual value.

When we went on a picnic though or had a church outing at the state park, the conflicting rules of multiple families muddied the waters of what was allowed by God. Enjoying nature was approved, as everyone in the Bible enjoyed nature, but what if that led to a park with a swimming pool, or a field with a baseball pitch, or a track with a finish line? Could we enjoy nature if it might stir up feelings of competitiveness and distract from the beauty of God's creation? One alternative to swimming was wading, which quieted complaints from even the most stringent Adventists. I could walk in the water, preferably not too deep, in respect for what weren't written rules, but more like divine barometers by which families could measure their holiness. When it came to games and sports, the same principles applied. There weren't set rules, but the bigger your sacrifice, the further you were from sin, and the closer you were to God.

As a kid, my job was to find the loopholes. I became a pro at finding Christian-themed games that were actually just regular games with some biblical element tacked on. Six days a week I played freeze tag, where when someone tagged me, I was frozen until someone else tagged me free. But on the Sabbath, I played *Bible* freeze tag, so when someone tagged me, I was frozen until I said a Bible verse and *then* someone tagged me free. Six days a week I played charades, but on the seventh day we played *Bible* charades.

Christian-based games were sold in stores as altered versions of popular, non-religious ones. My personal favorite was called *Egypt to Canaan*, which was like Old Testament Trivial Pursuit, but your game pieces traveled the path of Moses and the children of Israel out from Egypt and through the desert, surviving on manna sent from heaven and water that poured from rocks until you reached the promised land. Trivia questions moved your pieces forward, and I had to learn the Old Testament fast if I ever wanted to win. My brother and I memorized answers from the trivia cards to race ahead in hopes that a Chance card wouldn't set us backwards with an act of unrighteousness. Chance cards were like, "you doubted God, move back two spaces," or "you built a false idol, move back four spaces," or "God commanded you to collect manna only after sunset and you lost faith, built an altar, and sacrificed a cow, move back to start."

I built a deep appreciation for a genre of entertainment that was embraced by a small audience of kids who were raised, even if only one day a week, on Christian adventures. Little known to the less-religious families, there were Christian adaptations of everything imaginable across cassette tapes, videos, books, and music. *Veggie Tales*, *Adventures in Odyssey*, and *The Greatest Adventure: Stories from the Bible* were great, and better than nothing on the Sabbath. I listened to *Adventures in Odyssey's* tales of John Avery Whitaker and the small town of Odyssey, full of daring and thoughtful young people coming of age. I listened to *Jungle Jam and Friends'* silly antics in the animal kingdom that always came with a funny song and a moral. "God only made one you. Not 20, not 10, not two. In all of the whole world through…God only made one you."

Cassettes were played and rewound endlessly on Saturdays. They were like a Christian Disney, so much fun that sometimes, if only for an hour or two, we forgot we were following rules at all. Since my parents were divorced and every other Sabbath was spent with our dad, Darryl and I got to play Bible-based video games on our newly acquired and obsessed-over Sega Genesis when the board games wore out. We had one game called *Exodus* and another named *Joshua & the Battle of Jericho*. They were essentially the same game, with puzzles where you moved rocks up, down, left, or right and avoided magicians and other evils, and they were nearly impossible for a child to beat, like the other impossibly hard video games we were getting used to. Both were clones of Nintendo's popular *Boulder Dash*, but small details would make a regular 16-bit video game into a *Christian* 16-bit video game for more relaxed parents like my dad. Moses shot W's at enemies, meant to signify the word of God. The background music pieces were digitized versions of popular children's hymns like "Father Abraham." There was Old Testament trivia between each level that would earn manna. Not "points." Manna.

Christian playtime was secretly fun, despite the growing realization of the chasm between my Adventist upbringing and that of the kids I would play with outside. When the sun set on Friday night, ushering in the Sabbath, we would turn off the TV while other kids would keep watching. When we woke up Saturday morning, I would get ready for church while other kids would get ready for Saturday morning cartoons.

I'd still watch cartoons, but on that one day a week my cartoons would be different than theirs. Bible-based cartoons were my quintessential Sabbath afternoon pastime, where my morality, values, and character would be reinforced outside of church and inside my family's comfort zone. I resented the Sabbath for taking away *X-Men: The Animated Series* and *The Tick*, but the resentment only lasted a few minutes after Friday's sunset when those cartoons were replaced with *Veggie Tales*.

"If you like to talk to tomatoes, if a squash can make you smile, if you like to waltz with potatoes, up and down the produce aisle...have we got a show for you." I would repeatedly sing the name *Veggie Tales* over and over again, jumping and dancing as Bob the Tomato, Larry the Cucumber, Junior Asparagus, and all the other characters flashed through the intro montage of their adventures. I would sing Silly Songs with Larry and memorize songs about how "God is bigger than the boogieman, he's bigger than Godzilla or the monsters on TV. Oh, God is bigger than the boogieman, and he's watching out for you and me."

Alongside *Veggie Tales* were less commercially popular, more obscure cartoons that came before it and helped pave the way for its success. *The Greatest Adventure: Stories from the Bible* was one of them, produced by Hanna-Barbera and starring a group of young, modern-day friends who relived Bible stories in each episode. The show's introduction explained the set-up each time, as two young archeologists, Derek and Margo, along with their friend Moki, were on a dig when the sand began to swirl under their feet. The quicksand pulled them under as they crashed to a floor underneath in a cloud of dust obscuring everything in a strange room.

"And as the dust settles, they stare up in awe at a vast chamber, filled with giant relics and artifacts from another civilization," said the narrator. The three of them looked to the end of the chamber to see a door, and before they knew it the door opened to transport them to another time, an era from the Bible, where I relived a famous story through the perspectives of these three young people who watched Biblical history unfold in front of their eyes.

The Greatest Adventure: Stories from the Bible ran from 1986 to 1992, releasing thirteen 30-minute episodes. There was a smart, outspoken woman in Margo, a dark-skinned jokester in Moki, and an upright, classic good guy in Derek. The one Black character, Moki, was the only non-archeologist in the bunch, oddly referred to only as "their nomad friend," and he was used mostly for comic relief. Still, he was there, making me laugh as the Bible's class clown and the earliest Black animated character I can recall.

I would quote lines from my favorite episodes with Darryl, our favorite being the taunts of the Philistine Goliath. "A stick?" Goliath asks David, after days of leading the Philistines each morning in their threats against the children of Israel. "Am I a dog that you commeth to me with a stick?" Goliath's evil confidence was captivating, earning him the endearment that would group him with the likes of Pharaoh and Megatron, blending my Biblical nerddom with the secular. Goliath's challenge had first been made plainly over a month prior, at the moment he appeared on a distant hilltop with his goons behind him, leaving the Israelites aghast.

"Israelites! Send out a man who dares fight me. If he kills me, all Philistines will be your servants." The Israelites mumbled in agreement. "But," Goliath added, "if I kill him, all Israelites will be our slaves." The mumbles faded, and King Saul was left with a choice. The Israelites could wage war and risk the death of many, or they could put all their faith in one individual battle and save countless lives. Only no one would step up to fight Goliath, a fact that led to his daily taunting.

"Come! Come! I grow lonely out here," he yelled at the audience of cowards. "Surely, amongst the men of Saul, there is one man with spine. Step forth!" Every weak-hearted Israelite in that camp looked at each other, and then down at the ground, ashamed, until Goliath yelled his final instructions and my first introduction to the schoolyard bully. "I shall return tomorrow, and every day thereafter, until you send forth a warrior to meet me." With that, Goliath stabbed his spear into the ground to mark the spot he would return each day to take the Israelite's lunch money. Goliath was the original Cell from *Dragon Ball Z*, waiting in the same spot just daring someone to run his fade.

But David was in the audience one day, and patiently waited for a track to explode on after hearing Goliath's threat. Goliath had pointed at Israelite men one by one, asking if they would be the one to step to the throne, laughing at each prospect. The Israelite men looked at the ground one by one, afraid and embarrassed of being called out with no intention of standing up for themselves. But there's always one kid who isn't afraid of the schoolyard bully, and that was David.

"Why does no one fight him?" David asked. "Who is this Philistine who defies you?"

"Goliath of Gath," his brother, responded. "He has made this challenge every day."

"For how long?" David asked. He was expecting it was one day of cowardice, maybe two. A week would be unfathomable.

"The past forty days," his brother replied, and that shit nearly broke David. David was like, "Forty days? Forty days, like the whole time Noah was on the boat? Forty days like Moses on Mount Sinai? Forty days, like how long we took to spy out Canaan? Forty, are you fucking kidding me?" His brothers were angry and embarrassed, made worse when David chastised them for not standing up to fight against their oppressor.

"You have no right to talk so big. You know nothing of fighting, only tending sheep. Why did you come here anyway? You wanted to peek out from behind a tree and see a battle?"

David looked around. Do you see a fucking battle here? "But I see no battle," he yelled. "Only one lone enemy who dishonors us. If no one else fights the Philistine, I will."

"You?" his brothers said.

"Yes, and gladly," David responded. And he did. After convincing King Saul to put him on the court, David came out the next morning with no armor, no sword, just the shepherd gear he wore to work in the morning. Goliath was fucking disgusted.

"For your insolence," Goliath taunted David, "I will carve your flesh and feed it to the fowls of the air and the beasts of the field." But David stood defiant.

Since there weren't many new Christian features coming on a regular basis, the episodes played on repeat each Sabbath, part of their entertainment value coming from just how well I knew each line of dialogue. That was the nature of my childhood for one day each week, a whole world of faith-based media whose content was different from what I watched the other six days, but with an obsession equally sincere as I accepted its consolation. They weren't Saturday morning cartoons, and I knew well enough to keep them a secret.

CHAPTER 4

FROM SABBATH TO SUNDAY

In my grandma's house I shared a bedroom with Darryl that had a thin wall between our room and grandma's. It mostly meant that we could hear the news and *The Price Is Right* coming from her TV, but one night, when I wet the bed after insisting to myself that I would stop, the thin wall served another purpose.

I was angry at myself for having wet the bed, and I wanted the comfort of my grandma, but I also had a deep fear of Lucifer. I knew he lived in the dark, and I often felt that he stood in the doorway of my bedroom peering in on me at night, or that he lived in the shadows between the lights that danced on the ceiling when the reflection of a car's headlights found its way upstairs through my bedroom window, or that he would reach up slowly from under my bed and touch my foot if only I were foolish enough to leave that foot exposed to his touch.

God was omnipotent, omniscient, and omnipresent, more powerful than the devil, but the night belonged to Satan. And though I could repeat Bible verses in my mind, telling myself that the Lord was my shepherd, that I walked through the valley of the shadow of death, that I would fear no evil, and that my rod and my staff would comfort me, I still feared the figure I could make out when my eyes adjusted to the darkness, the one that stood motionless in the doorway, the one that rarely moved or made a sound. It was his silence that terrified me most.

The devil obstructed the path between me and my grandma as I lay covered in piss, too afraid to move but equally frustrated that I was still wetting the bed at all. Every night I would have the same dream and it wasn't fair. I would dream that I stood up, walked to the bathroom, and stood over the toilet. Only after I felt the warmth spread over my body would I realize that I was still asleep and in bed, a trick played on me with no bully or trickster to blame but myself.

I began to cry in hopes that grandma would hear me. Darryl slept soundly through the crying as planned, but grandma hadn't woken up yet either, so after five minutes, I began to cry louder. After ten minutes, louder still. Eventually I leaned up in bed and wailed, sending the message that I wouldn't tire out, that I wouldn't go quietly in the night.

The door cracked open, and my grandma stepped in. She asked what was wrong and I told her my frustrations, that I had wet the bed again, that I had the dream that tricked me, and she listened, got me changed, and put me back to sleep. There was a reliability in her comfort, knowing that if I cried long enough or loud enough, she would hear me and eventually give me a hug. When my mom was swayed by non-denominational Evangelicals to leave the Seventh-day Adventist church in lieu of theirs, I would learn the wall went both ways.

The first time I went to church on Sunday was at a non-denominational church outside the city. It was racially diverse, and after being introduced to the Black couple who brought my mom into the church, I made friends with their daughter, who was a dark-skinned girl a year or two older than me, and with a few other kids she introduced me to in her Sunday School class. It was my first time attending "Sunday School" after years of "Sabbath School," and it felt like an act of rebellion, despite my having no choice in being there.

I knew of Sunday School from the TV and movies, and from the kids out in "the world," who were somehow still of "the world" despite being in a church precisely because their church didn't honor the Sabbath. Their church had tepid Christians, the lukewarm church of Laodicea, the type who would choose which commandments to follow and would disregard the fourth. But here I was, in Sunday School myself.

I had never heard of "non-denominational" before, so I struggled to make sense of them not belonging to a particular group. It didn't make sense that they didn't have a defined set of beliefs. Their denomination was the absence of a denomination, yet here they were, paradoxically as a group. I began to define non-denominational for myself in the only way I knew how, by beginning to memorize what I heard in Sunday School and tying the concepts back to what I already knew.

The broad strokes were the same. God has three parts, the Father, the Son, and the Holy Spirit, Jesus is God's son who died for our sins, Satan wishes for our destruction, Noah survived the flood, and Moses rescued the Children of Israel. I found there were other concepts that were foreign, though, but not necessarily incompatible, like when I learned about iniquities. At first, I thought "iniquity" was a different word for "sin", used by this denomination that called itself non-denominational, but iniquities were different, a type of moral failing that I learned was transferrable. Iniquities like alcoholism or a cursing tongue could be passed down from parents to children. In fact they *would be* passed down unless they were stopped, making it a moral obligation not only for the individuals themselves but also for their children to follow.

At first blush it struck me as unfair, but it was also how things worked. I could cite countless times in the Bible where God punished a family for the sins of an individual, so it made sense that the only way to stop an iniquity was to face it and overcome it, to keep it from being passed on. But I understood it best from a movie I had become infatuated with, one that explained the transfer of a generational curse through a young boy who was stalked by another young boy. The movie came out in 1993 when I was 8 years old, and a copy of it found its way into our home a few years later, as if by magic. It was *Dragon: The Bruce Lee Story.*

It was the martial arts that pulled me in, of course. Bruce Lee would stand against half a dozen goons at a time, his high-pitched battle cries sporadically darting through the air with the speed of his kicks. He was handsome, charming, powerful, and heroic. But it was his demon that captured me.

Bruce was stalked by a generational curse that was personified as a demon that could appear without warning. No one could see the demon except Bruce, and he thought no one would believe him if he'd explained what he saw. But Bruce's father, Hoi-chuen Lee, was well-acquainted with the demon. It had stalked him too, and his father before him. The demon had claimed the first-born boys of their family line, one by one, a walking manifestation of what each of them had failed to overcome.

Bruce's first encounter with the demon was carved in my memory from the first time I saw it. A little boy my age was walking home alone in the dark. Statues lined the sides of the path he needed to walk, and he feared the same thing I would

44

have feared, that any one of them could open its eyes, step in front of me and claim me for its own. He closed his eyes, as I would have done, before realizing he couldn't walk with his eyes closed. He opened his eyes, as I would have done, and looked meekly at the figures that horrified him. And he began to run, as I would have done, when he thought he heard one of them rumble, because waiting to be sure wasn't worth the risk.

I recognized what he would see next, a dark silhouette in a dark room. It stood over the foot of my bed at night, or sometimes sat in a corner, or stood blocking the doorway that would be my exit. It blocked Bruce's path now, walking slowly towards him in the alleyway because walking faster would suggest it was concerned with his escape. But you and it both knew that it was in control and that there would be no escape, except to wake up from a dream. And you so desperately wished it *was* a dream.

It was Hoi-chuen Lee who woke from the dream, though. And it was Hoi-chuen Lee who had a plan.

"Kung Fu is more than a system of fighting," Bruce was told in his first training montage as he slowly hit the Mu ren zhuang, the wooden Wing Chun dummy. "It's a system of thought." I counted the hits as he struck, one…two…three, the combo growing faster as he grew older until it was one, two, three, and then one-two-three, and then finally a rapid onetwothree. "You must outthink your opponent, whatever form he takes. Because some of them will be more than just men."

"What else could they be, sifu?" Bruce asked his Wing Chun teacher.

"We all have inner demons to fight. We call these demons fear and hatred and anger. If you don't conquer them, then a life of a hundred years is a tragedy. If you do, a life of a single day can be a triumph."

After losing his firstborn son to the demon, Hoi-chuen Lee had first tried to trick the demon from pursuing Bruce. He gave him a girl's name, Sai-fong, and dressed him in dresses as a child to keep the demon from knowing he had another son. "I made you speak English, all so we could fool him," Hoi-chuen Lee told an adult Bruce as he explained the truth of the demon. "But now he knows. And he's coming for you."

When Bruce was sent to America to escape the demon, he was excited, and his glowing optimism was captured in the belly of a shipping boat as he interrupted an older Chinese man from reading his newspaper.

"I've always wanted to go to America," Bruce told him. "James Dean. French fries. The sky's the limit, that's what they say."

"Not a Chinaman's chance," the man replied. "They say that, too. You ever hear that?"

"No," Bruce said. The man folded his newspaper and made time for the bright-eyed boy who wanted to practice his English.

"You know, the Chinese, we built the railroads there," he said. "The Americans, the gwailo, would lower Chinamen over the cliff in baskets to set the dynamite. Get pulled up too slow? *Bang!*" he said to Bruce, who was realizing this wasn't a happy story about James Dean, or French fries, or the sky being the limit. "Rope break? *Bye-bye*," the man said softly. "*Bye-bye*," he repeated, his gaze now softer than his voice, as if he was looking into a dark mine. "*Bye-bye*," he said, a third time. "Americans say 'not a Chinaman's chance.' And round-eyed gwailo would laugh."

The older man paused for a moment, as if to reflect on his own experiences, the same experiences he expected

Bruce would have with racism, and on the sorrow of dimming a young man's hopes but feeling that the responsibility outweighed the discomfort. He looked Bruce in the eye when he said, "We're not human to them," and Bruce met his eyes with the defiance of a man set to prove someone wrong.

"How do you know?"

"I'm a history teacher," the man replied, and went back to his newspaper.

Of course, the man was right in his foreshadowing of Bruce's experiences in America, and on the evolution of an optimistic boy who would later rant about his worthlessness in America, that he was little more to them than Mickey Rooney's racist depiction from *Breakfast at Tiffany's*. "They got such a good line of bullshit!" Bruce would yell. "*Come and get it! America, the mountain of gold, it's for everybody!* Yeah, it's for everybody white. But they don't tell you that."

Bruce had fallen in love with a white woman, Linda, who became his wife, and Bruce's boiling point came when she urged them to move back to the U.S. after he'd left to become a star in Asia. "Back there, I'm just another gook. Just another wetback, Charlie Chan, slopehead, coolie dishwasher in a stinky chinky restaurant. *Wash your shirt, mister white man? Please? No tickee, no shirtee! Order one from column A and one from column B. Me happy to build the railroads. Me happy to build the mines for you, mister white man.* Is that who I am? Is it? Tell me. Tell me that's who I am!"

But that would come later.

"Things are different now," Bruce smiled at the historian with what would become a trademark cheerfulness that he would show against racism to come, an optimism that would be eroded to its breaking point. "I'm different. I am, you'll see."

Since I hadn't yet recognized racism in my own young life, the anti-Asian racism that Bruce faced didn't resonate as much as its effects did. In my own way I recognized their effects though. The fear, the anger, and the hatred that haunted him. Their effects were like those of the demon, like the iniquity I was trying to understand in my new church, that would be passed down if unconquered. And *Dragon: The Bruce Lee Story* ended as it began, with Bruce face to face with the demon.

Only this time he wasn't a boy. After his father's death in 1965, Bruce returned to China for his funeral and met again with Ip Man, his sifu, the man who had taught him Wing Chun and about demons when Bruce was a child. He was the second person Bruce had told about his demon, and the second person to believe him.

"When your father first brought you here, he told me everything," Bruce's sifu said. "He wanted you to learn Wing Chun to protect yourself against man, and other forces."

"I thought that was all superstition," Bruce confessed.

"Superstition is a name the ignorant give to their ignorance. You were special then, and you're special now. *That's* why the demon wants you."

But Bruce was intimidated in a way he hadn't been with each prior fight, those fights against men. It showed in his face and in what he asked next, "What if I won't fight him?"

"You have no choice. You're fighting for more than yourself."

"What are you saying, sifu?" Bruce asked.

"As I told you, this demon is your inner fear. It doesn't matter how many men you defeat. If you don't conquer your own fears, your will pass your demons onto your children, as your father passed his onto you."

And when the demon came next, it was a young Brandon Lee, a boy who looked like the young Bruce in the alley, who incited his father into action. The demon had been crushing Bruce in a cemetery at night in the pouring rain. It had been indomitable as it flung Bruce's body through the darkness and pounded Bruce's face into his own headstone. But when Brandon began screaming for his dad, the demon heard it and knew there was a new son. And when it dropped Bruce to walk towards his son Brandon, Bruce stood up. He ran to his crying son. He told him to run. He told him it would be okay.

And he kicked the demon in its fucking throat.

The demon staggered back, its first sign that it could feel pain. It paused to look at Bruce, the man who stood before it on a staircase between two dragon statues, ready to fight. Then it grew spikes on its face to keep from being struck again.

Sliding nunchucks from the mouth of one of the stone dragons, Bruce swung that thing in protection of his son. The demon leaned back and forth like it was waiting for an opening in Double Dutch. It took a step. Thwap! Bruce hit him in the throat with the nunchucks for the first time. The demon tried to kick. Thwap, thwap! Bruce struck twice more, now we're up to three in total. Parry, thwap-thwap! Parry, thwap! Seven, eight, nine! By the tenth hit the demon nearly fell but gathered its strength for one last push. The demon ran towards Bruce, who flipped over it, and wrapped the nunchucks around its throat. Bruce screamed into the rain and the darkness, and his screams mixed with the echoes of the languished cries that followed the demon wherever it went.

Bruce protected his son. He defeated his curse.

I kept learning the principles of my new, non-denominational church, though grandma didn't approve of mom leaving our Adventist church, even for another church, and especially of her taking us kids with her. A non-Seventh-day Adventist church might as well have been atheism to grandma. She and mom argued over doctrine, over mom's decision to take her children to this new church, and over what would come of our souls if she continued on her path.

But mom stood her ground. She stood her ground against dad, and now again against her mother. She had fight in her, and though it wasn't often there, it was strong whenever she needed it, so when grandma gave her an ultimatum of either leaving that church or leaving her house, mom chose the latter. For the first time since my parents' divorce, we were packing up and moving out on our own.

One night before we left, Darryl and I were asleep in our shared bedroom when I woke up from the sound of talking from the other side of the wall. I ignored it at first, until it grew loud enough to be unignorable. It was grandma, who was speaking to God. Not speaking but crying. Not crying but wailing. It was biblical wailing, the kind of Mordecai and David, of sackcloth and ashes, of the tearing of clothes and of intercessory prayer.

Grandma begged God to save her daughter, and as if God had said no, that her daughter was too far gone, her wailing escalated to begging God for forgiveness. Her cries were mixed with Bible verses of how God promised in 1 Corinthians 10:13 to not put more upon her than she could bear, that he would always make an escape from her turmoil, but oh Lord, why?

I listened to my grandma from the other side of the wall pleading with God on my mom's behalf. I wanted to help her, to comfort her the way she had comforted me, but I was also scared of the dark and of the devil who lived in it, and of the spiritual war on the other side of the wall where he was undoubtedly present in his final push to break my grandma and claim her daughter's soul.

Finally, I fell asleep in the comfort of a promise I made to myself that I would never leave God's church. If I couldn't defeat a demon, I would at least keep grandma from crying out to God on my behalf.

CHAPTER 5

THE BLACK FISH WHO SANG

We were homeless for a stretch, but I didn't realize it until my mom started to cry in the driveway of my childhood home, 17164 Braille, the rundown 750 square foot house where I used to pour orange juice in my oatmeal. It was where we lived back when my parents were together, and although I understood that my mom was asking my dad for a favor by being there, I didn't understand how hard that was or how desperate we were to squat in the old home he couldn't sell.

We had a dog, a rambunctious Labrador that we named Sox because of her white paws, which Darryl and I had cried and begged for until our mom and grandma had let us keep her. We had bought her for $50 from a random house that had set a sign on their brown lawn that read "puppies for sale," and now my mom was out on her own, responsible for two kids and a dog. We put Sox in an old crate in the living room along with the few belongings we had, but she kept breaking out so we couldn't leave to go run the errands my mom needed to do that day. Every time we'd reach the door, Sox would wriggle free from her crate and run to join us. Finally, we used some stray rope to tie up the gaps in between the bent crate bars and we made it inside the car. Mom took a deep breath behind the steering wheel, started the engine, and was almost able to shift into reverse before seeing the window blinds torn down and flung across the living room, and an enthusiastic Sox jumping freely at the window. That's when she burst into tears.

My mom had a best friend named Shirley who lived with her husband, Lukas, across the tunnel in Windsor, Ontario. Shirley invited us to live with them until we were back on our feet, and so we moved to Canada. I was excited by the change, instantly noting the differences between Windsor and Detroit as we commuted daily across the two countries to get to school. We lost our car so we used Shirley's to get to school, and we presented a hand-written letter each morning and afternoon at immigration hoping to explain why a Black family with an American passport was driving a car with Canadian plates. We made a game of it each day, taking turns guessing which customs official would be understanding, and which would step outside their booth, put a sticker on our car, and ask us to pull to the left and step inside for questioning. We left an hour early each morning just in case.

The commute was like a portal between two realms. We drove into the tunnel from Canada, and when we emerged there was downtown Detroit, then I-75 to the Jeffries Freeway on our way to school. On the way back, we might take the Ambassador Bridge back to Canada. On one side was the familiar working-class struggle of hard-working Detroit, on the other was the charming ease of affluence that was given on loan from Shirley and Lukas.

Shirley was a white woman with a round face. She had blonde hair that was cut in a bob that reminded me of white pastors' wives. Lukas was Greek, wore a thick moustache, and was covered with dark hair. Both were friendly and kind, and they thought the world of Darryl and me. They praised us for being such good kids, but otherwise they left us alone to play outside or watch TV in their finished basement where we stayed. We weren't given chores to do, nor could I see any of my friends, so I took to walking around Windsor.

I would walk around with nowhere to go, able to come and go without keys to Shirley and Lukas' house because people in Canada didn't lock their doors. They would give me spending money that made me feel rich, five dollars here or ten dollars there. When I was given American money, I would spend more time enjoying the calculations of what I could buy with the exchange rate than I would actually spending it. There were parks and green grass and small bookstores that carried comics, and I roamed aimlessly with money in my pocket until I found the small arcade that would be my afterschool and weekend playground for the next few months. I exchanged my dollars into tokens, winning a bonus two tokens for each American dollar, and sampled the games until I landed on a new arrival, *Darkstalkers*, where I would spend as long as I could playing the 2D fighting game until I would run out of money and go home and watch cartoons.

None of my Detroit friends knew I was living in Canada, and I assumed Darryl's didn't either. I was simultaneously excited and embarrassed about it, recognizing the fun I was having that came as consequence of our poverty, and fearing that if my friends found out they would make fun of me. Darryl was one of the most popular kids in school, meaning he had more to lose, and I didn't need to be told not to jeopardize his standing with talk about Canada, just like I didn't need to be told not to talk about knowing Bible verses by heart. Living in the suburbs would be bad enough, let alone across the bridge in Canada. Instead, our Detroit lives continued as normal when we were in Detroit, playing basketball and football on the playground, laughing raucously in the cafeteria, trying to fit in with my older brother and his cool, older friends after school as they argued about who would win in a fight, until my mom picked us up and drove us back to Canada. I loved those arguments, watching them yell vehemently, animatedly, appearing angry to anyone who didn't know them but full of joy to anyone who did.

Before Canada, I had been quiet when my brother's friends let me spend time with them after school, feeling a mix of intimidation by their age and honor that they allowed me to sit with them at all in the cafeteria or in empty classrooms where we technically weren't supposed to be, but those months in Canada became something like my nerd origin for me. I spent so much time between the arcade, bookstore, and Shirley and Lukas' basement that when we were in school and Darryl's older friends would argue about which character would win in a fight, I had an opinion. An informed one.

I remember the first time I was included in the conversation when someone argued who would win in a random fight, and they asked if I watched Tommy become the White Ranger. My thought was *who hadn't*?

To hop in the ring, you had to be ready with statistics and specific references. Boy, girl, young, or old, if you knew your shit, you knew your shit, and suddenly I knew my shit. Even better, waking up early for an international commute and watching Canadian channels meant sometimes stumbling on cartoons and episodes that were obscure. Better still, cartoon knowledge came naturally, like when I was asked the scientific name for cats and I'd already learned it from watching Felix because I was earnestly infatuated.

Coinciding with my budding identity as a nerd was noticing that there was another difference between the two ends of my commute. Windsor was white.

I was too small to experience overt racism, or too young to notice it even if I had, but I did notice that Darryl and I were the only Black kids wherever we went when we wandered about around our new home. If I were alone, I may have felt insecure, but given that Darryl didn't have friends in Windsor he was spending more time with me, and spending time with my older brother made me feel cool. I felt special even, like one half of a pair of characters who found themselves in a strange place. *Who would we be?* I wondered. We were two travelers on an adventure, like...like...like *who*?

That's when I started to search for Black characters like us. And as it turned out, my friends at school were doing it, too. Everyone was.

I wasn't just a nerd. I was a *Black* nerd. A subculture within a subculture rooted in a single implicit understanding that Black kids knew which characters were Black. Not just the actual Black characters like Storm, Static, Cyborg, Penny, Bebe's kids, or Geordi, but the characters who weren't Black, but somehow were, like Piccolo, Panthro, Ursula, Martian Manhunter, Demona, Lieutenant Worf, Sebastian the Crab, and a host of others who were widely chosen, without conspiracy or collaboration, as Black.

Characters on the border of our implicit rules of racial coding were invited into the family, as if ties in a racial tug-of-war were awarded to the minority by default. Take Nightcrawler. He was born Kurt Wagner from Germany, but his status as a misunderstood outcast with a heroic heart earned him the adoration of Black kids as much as his purple skin and racial ambiguity. With his mother as the blue shapeshifter

Mystique and his father the red demon Azazel, Nightcrawler and characters like him were chosen as ours so long as no proof existed that they were white.

Or take Gaia, from *Captain Planet*. She was the spirit of Earth who represented the peace and harmony of the planet. She varied in skin tone from episode to episode, even scene to scene, ranging from copper-skinned to olive, from purple eyes to blue, from blue hair to black, from the voice of Whoopi Goldberg to that of white Canadian actress Margot Kidder. Gaia's racial ambiguity was indicative of the time, edging towards diverse representation with a racially ambiguous Mother Earth as the spiritual guide of five Planeteers representing five continents of origin. If Gaia could have gone in either direction between white or Black, though, young Black America was happy to claim her as ours.

In everything I saw, I found Black characters where they didn't exist. Their experiences were so familiar to the Black experience that the Black characters became only obvious. They were outsiders, feared despite their contributions and heroism, misunderstood yet persevering. Or they were resourceful, able to thrive with the deck stacked against them, or they were wise beyond their years, or they were dripping with confidence in who they were despite that identity being different from what was accepted or expected. Or they were all these things rolled in one, written as a poem on faded pages of the Black diaspora.

Though many were white, some of the voice actors were Black in real life, because a majority of white producers and casting directors either intentionally influenced our mental gymnastics of cultural connection, or they unintentionally made the same connections we were making as kids. Our magic was the skill of positive attribution, an almost reverse appropriation, ascribing our strongest, sincerest, and most vulnerable characteristics to the avatars we needed to mirror our humanity.

It was an adaptation born out of necessity, an ability to counteract other depictions we had been shown in animation that were grotesque reflections in a house of horrors. Onscreen media would eventually transition from this more blatantly demeaning imagery, but there was still much of it to be found lingering into the 90s, subtler but still very much present.

From the 1930s to 1960s was the first golden age of animation, as the medium advanced to include the synchronized sound of the '20s and to introduce color in the '30s. The introduction of both sound and color was one of the Warner Brothers' earliest successes, leading to the familiar circles and technicolor backdrop we recall from shows like *Merry Melodies*, *Looney Tunes*, and later, *Tiny Toon Adventures*, perhaps with the words "That's all, folks!" splashed across its center. But the '30s also saw the first cartoon character to surpass Felix the Cat's popularity, courtesy of Walt Disney's newly colored mouse, Mickey. Warner Brothers and Disney were in an arms race of creating recognizable characters who could become cartoon superstars, and they were both learning that telling stories was the way to do it. Mickey brought his squad with him, and Porky Pig did, too.

Mickey Mouse, the anchor of the Disney gang, was soon followed by Pluto, Goofy, and Donald Duck, all in the 1930s. Warner Brothers had Porky Pig, followed by Daffy Duck, Elmer Fudd, and eventually Bugs Bunny, the character who surpassed all Warner Brothers' other characters in popularity, who was added in 1940. Other contenders included Fleischer Studios with Betty Boop and Popeye, and later

Metro-Goldwyn-Meyer's Tom and Jerry, and Terrytoon's Mighty Mouse, but they were less gangs than individual acts. Disney and Warner Brothers were in the empire business, building universes of popular characters from which everyone could choose their favorite. And as they both found comfort in their ability to write short comedic stories for popularity, they expanded to new settings to leverage fish-out-of-water comedy by introducing audiences to a strange new place and letting the laughs roll.

One of the results is what came to be known as the Censored 11. As 1930s innovation gave way to 1940s proliferation, Warner Brothers created 11 cartoons so racist that they are banned to this day as a stain in the memory of animation's expansion. In protection of their brand and now-iconic characters, Warner Brothers keeps the Censored 11 locked in the Warner Brothers vault with more security than Yacko, Wacko, and Dot. They are stricken from classic viewing marathons and cameo features because they reflect the accepted racism of the '30s, '40s, and '50s.

Uncle Tom's Bungalow is a take on *Uncle Tom's Cabin* and features watermelon-eating, tap dancing slaves on the auction block. *Jungle Jitters* has a white traveling salesman who tries to sell products to big-lipped Africans, only to find himself part of their cannibal stew. The depictions continue in *Coal Black and de Sebben Dwarfs*, *The Isle of Pingo Pongo*, and *All This and Rabbit Stew*, which features Bugs Bunny outwitting and mocking a slow-talking Black "coon" stereotype. Bugs later appears in the offensively titled, *Bugs Bunny Nips the Nips*, complete with a short, buck-toothed depiction of a Japanese soldier. The familiar catchphrase "What's up doc?" is followed by Bugs yelling a less familiar "Japs! Hundreds of them!" and outsmarting an army of heavily-accented Japanese stereotypes.

Racist animated depictions continued from the '30s and '40s to include full-length features, like when Disney joined in with perhaps its most prominent example in *Song of the South*. This was based on the book series that featured a character named Uncle Remus, the character on whom *The Boondocks'* Uncle Ruckus is based, *Song of the South* was released in 1946 from a $2-million budget, and it earned $65 million in revenue. Embarrassment of the film and its controversy outweighs its market success though, as to this day Disney declines to offer *Song of the South* for home release or availability on its streaming platforms. It remains one of the most searing and long-lasting racist depictions that Disney would rather leave forgotten, though it would hardly be Disney's last.

From Mickey Mouse's blackface in *Mellerdrammer* in the '30s, to the jive-talking crows in *Dumbo* in the '40s, to the Siamese cats *Lady and the Tramp*, *Aristocats*, and to *Chip 'n Dale's Rescue Rangers* in the '50s, '70s, and '80s, racism was drawn into the frames of animation's history such that by the time I sat in front of the television, an adaptive trait had developed to help protect me from what I would see. I learned to filter it out, having the keen skill to disassociate the negative depictions from the larger media I loved. I ignored the Pokémon named Jynx and focused on Brock. I watched Sebastian sing "Under the Sea" and ignored the Black Fish who sang.

As I learned to implicitly assign race to fictional characters, I was unaware of that same ability, that part of an uncanny commonality among non-white kids who grew up without diverse representation, to automatically assign race to characters for whom race wasn't prescribed. It was a process that ran in my subconscious, scanning the menu of characters for the Black one. White kids were being taught to not see race, and I was learning the exact opposite.

Black-coded characters fell into three categories. First are the racially ambiguous or unhuman-colored humans, like *Captain Planet*'s Gaia. With brown or blue-tinted skin, I claimed these characters the moment they showed a familiar feature of the Black experience within a predominately white culture. They're often one of few characters with their complexion, sometimes the Black-best-friend archetype or token Black, like Disney *Doug*'s best friend, Skeeter.

The second category is the anthropomorphic animals, who are human-like but not so much as to have an explicit race, leaving them up for grabs to the kid in front of the TV screen. Elmo, Goliath, Ursula, Panthro, Goofy, Max, Scrappy Doo, Lola Bunny, both S.W.A.T. Kats, Knuckles, and every Maximal in *Beast Wars* was Black. Most Black-coded characters fell into this category.

The third category is made up of aliens like Optimus Prime, Martian Manhunter, Modo from *Biker Mice from Mars*, Alf, Worf, Marvin the Martian, and, of course, Piccolo.

Any familiar feature of Black culture would make characters like those an addition to my team of heroes, misfits, and friends who would help me to see myself onscreen. One of those features was a traumatic history like their planet being destroyed, and their "kind" then being rejected by the new society where the characters find themselves as strangers. These were the Piccolos and Martian Manhunters, refugees with hearts of gold despite their painful past. They were often exploited and treated poorly, but were written to respond with a code of honor above that of those around them.

Another identifying feature was stubborn pride in the face of a dominant culture. Trapped as outsiders within a culture that believed or behaved one way, the Black characters challenged that culture with an unabashed confidence in who they were. These were the Ursulas and Dinobots, those who saw their own value, dominant culture be damned. They shook off their rejection and lived as they were, more likely to lure others into their way of thinking than to abandon their sense of identity to fit in.

I'd previously watched the anime *Dragon Ball* on weekday mornings before school, watching as a young Goku flew on a cloud with his tail behind him, but when I started watching *Dragon Ball Z* after its American debut in 1996, I found my character. Darryl's favorite was Vegeta, the prince of all Saiyans, and I would be Piccolo.

After about six months in Canada, we saved enough money to move out of Shirley and Lukas' home and into a townhouse complex in a Detroit suburb called Southfield. It felt like the best of both worlds, not only being back in Detroit, but also in a townhouse complex that was luxury as we knew it. It had a basement, a main floor, and an upstairs with two bedrooms. The primary bedroom even had its own bathroom, one of two and a half bathrooms in our new home. I loved running up and down the staircase, which was a switchback or U-shaped staircase perfect for shooting Nerf darts around corners, and throwing pillows from cover, and running as fast as I could before grabbing the railing to swing arounds its curve.

We were hood rich, and we loved it enough to ignore that mom had begun anointing the kitchen cabinets with holy oil and speaking in tongues. Vegeta and I had other concerns, like running around the staircase corner with Sox chasing at our heels.

CHAPTER 6

CARRY THAT WEIGHT

Mom and grandma were still at odds, but Darryl and I still visited grandma's house often, and the adults would talk as we raided the refrigerator and cabinets for food and left the grownups to deal with grownup things while we watched *Robin Hood: Prince of Thieves*.

It had become our favorite movie to watch. I didn't know who owned it or how it came to find itself in my pile of rubbish in my grandma's den, but as if by magic, it was there when I was around 10 years old, and would become the first PG-13 movie I would watch on repeat until I memorized every line, like I'd done years before with *The Transformers: The Movie*.

I liked Robin, but I loved Azeem, the Great One.

Played by Morgan Freeman, Azeem met Kevin Costner's Robin of Locksley in a Jerusalem prison where guards were cutting off the hands of imprisoned thieves. When Robin's friend was called for his turn, Robin shoved his own hand on the chopping block, offering to sacrifice himself instead.

"This is English courage," he said. I had no idea what that meant, or anything about England, but I was captivated when he pulled back at the last second and started a prison escape. Prisoners screamed through the chaos of the riot as Robin tried to break the chains of a fellow prisoner. When they wouldn't break, he heard a voice behind him.

"You cannot save them, Christian. But you can save me." It was Azeem, Black and shiny in all his glory, tied with a mere rope to the wall behind him. Azeem was a Moor, ostracized and feared, so when Robin asked why he should save him he made a simple, compelling case, "If you do not, we are all dead men." And so it began that Robin saved Azeem's life, and Azeem made a vow to follow Robin on his path until he saved his life in return. He would be the Black best friend, but for me, he would be so much more.

A moral compass, sage, and fierce fighter, Azeem helped Robin by choice, all the while pointing out Robin's inferiority. When they returned to England, Robin rolled in the mud like an animal, and it was the first of many "what is this white nonsense?" moments written on Azeem's face. A moment later, when Robin tried to ditch Azeem by having sailors take him by force, Azeem put them in the dirt.

"No man controls my destiny," he said. "Especially not one who attacks downwind and stinks of garlic."

And that was just the beginning. Repeatedly it was made clear that Azeem was his intellectual superior. When Robin bragged about using mistletoe to seduce women, Azeem said "Where I'm from, Christian, we talk to our women. We do not drug them with plants." The first time Robin was attacked, Robin called for his help and Azeem chose to stay where he was. Robin was upset that his sidekick didn't help, as he hadn't yet learned that Azeem wasn't at his beck and call. Azeem wasn't magical, nor was he subservient. He was only fulfilling a vow, and he would do it on his own terms.

"You whine like a mule," Azeem said. "You are still alive."
It became the mantra for my brother and I whenever the other
would complain, whenever we faced anything challenge. *You
whine like a mule. You are still alive.*

You whine like a mule. You are still alive.

Time and again Azeem was the erudite warrior who
never begged for his humanity despite being surrounded
by those who wanted to rob him of it. His self-worth was
secure despite him being quite literally the only person of
color. He was Piccolo or Martian Manhunter made into
a live-action character. In one short scene, Robin's friend
Duncan complained of Moors and Saracens, and cursed them
as ungodly savages. Duncan was blind, so couldn't see that
Azeem was Black, and Robin had never clued him in.

"Azeem… what manner of name is that?" Duncan then
asked. "Irish? Scottish?"

"Moorish," Azeem replied.

I loved Azeem's constant annoyance at Robin's ignorance.
In one scene, keeping watch atop a village wall, Azeem saw
Nottingham's men riding towards the castle. "Look," Azeem
said, handing his homemade monocular to Robin. Looking
through the monocular, Robin jumped back, took a second
look with his naked eye at the soldiers riding hundreds of
yards away, and then tried the monocular again to understand the wizardly of it all. When he drew his sword and tried
pointing it at a soldier through the magnifying glass, Azeem
snatched the monocular and looked at him with what can only
be described as a combination of wonderment and disgust.

"How did your uneducated kind ever take Jerusalem?"
Azeem asked.

"God knows," Robin said. "God knows."

The best expressions of Azeem's subtle superiority came

from the times he was fed up enough to let Robin wallow in his own consequences. Once, Robin's merry men weren't so merry to see him as they walked up on Robin and Azeem. Robin had arrogantly attacked the Sheriff's men, and the Sheriff had retaliated by attacking their families. Robin was facing a potential mutiny, and Azeem got up and walked away.

"If it's fame you seek, Christian, I think you have it."

Azeem might as well have said, "Let me hop off this tree branch and move away from your ass until you learn."

Azeem helped women give birth and taught men to fight while making teaching moments out of any given encounter. From counselor to warrior to obstetrician to teacher, Azeem was the real MVP as far as I was concerned. He was lighting gun powder and walking atop castle walls. He gave speeches while wielding dual Saracen swords, inspiring the people, other people's people, to fight to be free men. I made a mental note to borrow his confidence, should I ever be a stranger in a strange land.

On weekends, though, I traded TV and movies for video games. Darryl and I spent every other weekend with our dad, per the custody agreement after my parents' divorce, meaning every other weekend I had access to my Sega Genesis and my dad's relaxed rules. My dad still honored the Sabbath despite my mom's rebellion though, so Darryl and I played video games relentlessly from Saturday evening after sunset, until it was time to go back home on Sunday.

I lost access to my Sega Genesis when I lost access to my father.

My dad, Darryl Calhoun Senior, grew up in Philadelphia the oldest of three brothers and one sister. He moved to Berrien Springs, Michigan to attend Andrews Adventist University where he met my mom but left college partway through, and the two of them got married in their early-mid-twenties, had my brother, and three years later had me. The terms of their divorce meant visitation rights every other weekend, and those weekends felt like holidays. My dad having such limited access to Darryl and me meant that each occurrence demanded an activity, so every other weekend a trip was planned to race go-karts, leave the city to go horse-back riding, or visit the arcade at Chuck E. Cheese with what felt like unlimited quarters.

That changed when my dad remarried a woman named Delores, who saw the escapades of middle grade children as inconvenient to her previously child-free lifestyle. My dad moved into Delores' house a block or two on the other side of 8-Mile, the northern border of Detroit, in a suburb called Oak Park. It was a small house, but nice in the way that suburban streets felt nice, with clean streets and upkept lawns. Darryl and I were to follow one rule in exchange for one reward. On visitation weekends, the bedroom was ours, and we weren't to leave it. Meals would be brought to the room, we would eat on the bed, and it even had a small bathroom. That bedroom would be our world and we weren't to infest the rest of the house or bother them, and in exchange, we were given a Sega Genesis. And we couldn't have been happier.

Ignoring our circumstances of being children restricted to a small room, Delores felt like more of an absent step-mother than an evil one. We adjusted to her rules as normal because we had no choice, because we didn't know how to question, and because we finally had a Sega Genesis. I knew it was wrong though, because Darryl and I had an unspoken pact that we wouldn't tell mom that our visitations were spent locked in a single bedroom from Friday night to Sunday after-noon, leaving only to go to church on the Sabbath.

Our interests were aligned. We wouldn't expose that we were locked in a room by our dad and his new wife, and we wouldn't be exposed for spending each waking hour playing video games.

We learned to leave the game volume running when we pressed our ears to the door to eavesdrop on dad and Delores' fights, which mostly consisted of Delores yelling at my dad and him asking her not to yell because we might hear them. Sometimes she yelled about us, and we would laugh at the mischief of our having left the confines of our room to explore the basement and unintentionally getting our dad in trouble.

"Dad's in trouble," we might say in the same classroom voice we'd use for someone being called to the principal's office, holding the last syllable of "trouble."

Once, we heard her smack our dad across the face, and listened to him calmly demand that she not hit him. Most times though we would ignore it for the Genesis, or to watch *King Arthur and the Knights of Justice*, or *Xena: Warrior Princess*, or *Macron-1*, or any other spoil we earned by keeping our mouths shut. Don't snitch, and don't ruin a good thing.

I built a special relationship with fighting games, but particularly *Super Street Fighter II: Turbo*. I would comb through GamePro magazine at bookstores like I'd learned to do back in Canada, memorizing combos and directional commands for special moves. We couldn't shoot a fireball or swing a dragon punch though. We mechanically went through the motions but couldn't figure out how to rotate our thumbs in a proper quarter circle around the directional pad.

Since I was the quintessential younger brother, Player 2, I expected Darryl to figure it out first. He would typically beat me, until one day I shot a fireball and it clicked. I tried it again, and it worked. And again. I was able to do it on purpose, and it didn't take long before I figured out how to land a dragon punch as well.

Street Fighter II had begun laying a foundation to influence the entire genre of fighting games, and it sparked what would become a proud badge of honor as a young gamer. For the first time, I could beat my brother at something. Player 2 was now Player 1.

I learned to fight with each of the characters in *Super Street Fighter II: Turbo*, beating the game with all of them. Countless other 2D fighter games launched as clones of the series, carbon copies like *Teenage Mutant Ninja Turtles: Tournament Fighters*, and if you were good at one of them, you were good at them all.

And while *Street Fighter II* was taking off in popularity at my dad's house, it was taking over with Black kids everywhere. It became a test of bravado, like the gamer version of street ball, until *Street Fighter II* ranked among the most common nerdy hip hop references next to metaphors about Optimus Prime.

I would talk trash in *Street Fighter II*, and I could usually back it up. It became my point of pride, to the point where sometimes it wasn't enough just to win. I wanted to ruin lives.

There were three ways to know I had broken someone's spirit. One, they accused you of cheating, two, they claimed their controller was broken, three, they cried. And I saw it all. I saw gangsters get religious playing in *Street Fighter II*. I felt alive by being merciless, by drinking the tears of someone who thought they could button mash their way to victory. With *Street Fighter II* I tasted evil, and it tasted good.

Inviting friends to play *Street Fighter II* became a go-to invitation, including when family, neighbors, or church friends would visit for a friendly night of video games on a

Saturday evening. They were fish swimming with a shark, and they had no idea what they were up against. When I pressed and picked up the controller, my eyes changed.

Family members could get murdered, too. I didn't care. I played with my two cousins, Gregory and Malcolm, who would anime-gasp when a night of *Street Fighter II* turned in a genjutsu that felt like a thousand years. I Itachi'd my own family and slaughtered the whole village. People narrowly survived with their dignity intact. Some wouldn't come to church the next Sabbath. Their parents said they were sick.

I felt like a champion until I played *Samurai Shodown* with Deshawn, my brother's best friend from church who leaned a bit more toward the street, who proceeded to beat my ass.

After losing a few rounds, there came a point where I thought I had it figured out. I told myself that I had enough, that I would win this time. And I meant it. It wasn't enough to tell myself of the turning tide, so I told Deshawn as well. I was done playing, and I wouldn't lose anymore.

He proceeded to beat my ass again as if nothing had changed.

After months of winning and building my nerd identity on being good at something, I couldn't emotionally handle the ass beating he gave me. I did the worst thing I could possibly do and accused him of cheating. Then I told him my controller was broken. And then I cried. They were frustrated tears too. They were the angry tears, where I tried to keep from crying and it only made my chest heave harder as snot ran down my nose. I broke all the rules, and it was the worst moment of my fighting game life.

I knew I deserved it. But either way, I absolutely loved it.

One weekend, Delores happened to be away, perhaps

visiting family, and Darryl and I drove with our dad to run errands in what was our closest iteration of the activity week-ends we'd had before their marriage. We drove and stopped here and there, making fun of the talk radio our dad insisted on, stopping for fast food and eating things we were only allowed to eat under his care.

Late in the evening, Darryl and I fell asleep, cuddled together in the back seat of the car. This would happen some-times when our dad would stop to visit a church member, go to the bank or post office, or otherwise spend time doing grown-up errands that were so boring that we begged to stay in the car, so when we were left in a parking lot we were only glad that it was dark and quiet, and that we didn't have to go with him.

Darryl woke up first, the shine from the flashlight and taps on the glass enough to coax him awake. He shook me awake, and I blocked the light with my eyes. It was white light at first, from a flashlight, then as my eyes adjusted, red and blue, then as my ears adjusted, yelling to move slowly, to get out the car and to keep our hands up.

I was aware that guns were pointed at me, and terrified, but more than that I was confused. I couldn't make sense of why the flashlight was shining in our eyes, why the police had my dad leaned against their squad car as they handcuffed him, why they were yelling at me. We were just sleeping.

After standing outside watching the spiral of the police lights, an officer in plain clothes and a badge around his neck asked Darryl and me if that was our dad. He said words I didn't understand, so I memorized the phrase I was told as something that was bad, something that you're not supposed to do, or you'll get in trouble, and my dad had gotten in trou-ble.

My Dad was let go, and when we got back in the car he drove us back home quietly, except to say, "Your mom doesn't need to know about this," to which we silently agreed.

We wouldn't snitch. We wouldn't ruin a good thing.

I don't know if Darryl knew what "solicitation of a prostitute" meant, or if he simply memorized the phrase like me, but when we got home, he burst into tears, hugging mom, and explained what happened. He was old enough to be more afraid of the guns pointed at him, and I wasn't upset because Darryl was my older brother and to me infallible, so instead I was confused again as to why we would accept the consequences to come.

It would be a few years before I was allowed to see my dad or spend weekends with him again, after a new man came into my mom's life, after my mom met a man named Cliff.

I just wanted to be with my dad and keep the Sega Genesis.

I'd stay in the room. I wouldn't tell a thing. I'd carry that weight.

CHAPTER 7

WAY OUT WHERE THE DANDELIONS GROW

I began to toggle between two other identities. In one, I was a nerd whose sense of purpose was based on connecting with others who loved the same cartoons, comics, and video games as I did. In the other, I was a Christian in a pious home where most of those same things were frowned upon, if not expressly forbidden. Media deemed unholy by church leaders ranged from the obscene variety of *The Simpsons*, *Ren & Stimpy*, and *Bevis and Butthead*, to the kind deemed outright satanic, like *Pokémon*, *Harry Potter*, and *Goosebumps*.

While my brother and I technically weren't allowed to watch shows like *The Simpsons*, we had the leeway that came from a single mother's dedication to the rules losing out to her exhaustion and a lack of resources to enforce them. When I woke up at six in the morning, my mother was getting ready for work while I sat in front of the TV screen watching any and every show I wanted. When I returned home after school, more of the same. She was either unaware, too tired, or both. It was in those hours, from six in the morning until the morning commute, and from three in the afternoon until she returned from work, that were unsupervised, free, and lawless.

They were also prime time cartoon hours where I found my pop culture education, the foundation on which my worldview was building. Outside of learning from school and church was an education that came from a screen. I spent so much time there that the world I saw onscreen often felt more normal than actual life. "Normal" was *Ronin Warriors* and *The Puzzle Place*. "Normal" was *Sailor Moon* and the Pizza Hut commercial that played before *Teenage Mutant Ninja Turtles*, where "I point to the sky and I look up above, and a baseball falls into my glove," and "that's why I play in right field, way out where the dandelions grow."

To be "normal" wasn't to be ordinary or common, the word held a different meaning to a kid who watched every other kid onscreen go on spectacular adventures. "Normal" meant finding Max's cap and discovering you were the Cap Bearer, or stumbling across a magical amulet as mummies come alive, or learning a secret about your family that reveals you to be a witch, or mutant, or magician, or literally anything but normal. Adventure was the "normal" I wanted.

I should have been careful what I wished for. As my mom leaned deeper into her new church, her focus shifted towards spiritual warfare. At first, she had brought us to church but let us keep our distance from fully participating in her new faith, but she had started to bring it home. At church, I was terrified as they cast out demons and spoke in tongues, anointing forehands and screaming at the devil, but now it was at home where we lived.

My mom began praying over us each morning and night, dipping her finger in a small vial of holy oil and marking a cross on our foreheads. It would ward off Satan's demons she told us, as she had us kneel at the foot of her bed and pray. Soon she began anointing everything in the house, including our dog Sox. From furniture to appliances to the helium balloons we brought home from a birthday party, she would light candles and pray and anoint them.

One day, Darryl and I were watching *The Simpsons* in our bedroom when she called for us to come into her room. We thought we were in trouble, maybe leaving the TV too loud so she heard a curse word or dirty joke, but it was less a scolding than a warning of her new gifts. She had learned from the church that God granted gifts to those who were righteous, and that those gifts were granted when someone was able to let the Holy Spirit flow through them. She had been studying for months for the occasion, something that seemed less like Bible study than a training regimen to reach a certain level of piety, a worthiness for the Holy Spirit to flow through her. The occasion had come, she told us, and she could now speak in tongues, and with it came her gift. She was able to sense the spirits in a room. And she knew we were watching something bad because there were three demons in our bedroom with us.

The demons petrified me. My mom seeing demons was confirmation of my worst fears. I had been too embarrassed to admit even to Darryl that there were malevolent spirits around me that I couldn't see. I *knew* they were there, I *knew* it. And now I wanted nothing more than to be wrong, to have my mom be wrong, to have them *not* be there or to have her cast them out.

But she couldn't cast them out, though. She wasn't strong enough for that, her gift was only to sense them, to count them, to know that they were there. She said that sometimes she was scared of them, too. Just the previous night she had awoken from her sleep, hearing a scratching sound downstairs in our apartment. The scratching sound continued for some time, growing closer and closer to her closed bedroom door. When the scratching stopped, whatever it was waited on the other side.

When she opened the door, there was a helium balloon floating in front of her. It was the balloon we'd gotten from a birthday party, one that she knew was possessed or moved by the devil, she explained, because of our staircase. There was no wind and no windows near the staircase, but the balloon had to climb from downstairs along the ceiling of our switch-back staircase, turn, and then float in the opposite direction before making its way down the hallway to wait outside her door.

After explaining her gift, she asked Darryl and me to kneel before her. When we did, she took out her vial of oil, anointed our foreheads, and began to pray. She prayed for our sight, oh God, to recognize the sin that would lead us astray. She prayed for light, dear Lord, to guide our path. She prayed for protection, oh God, against the devil who stalks like a roaring lion seeking whom he may destroy. Her speech grew faster and louder as Darryl and I knelt before her, my eyes clenched tight.

It came suddenly then, my mom speaking in a language I didn't understand. It sounded almost like she was gargling water, but with clearer syllables and alliterations that danced across the alphabet. It was the first time I heard her speaking in tongues, and I thought she was possessed by demons. I considered running away, but Darryl was there, too, and I had nowhere to run, so I stayed. I stayed and I clenched my eyes tight, and I never looked at her when she spoke in tongues, not once. I would close my eyes and wait for it to be over.

Fortunately, my mom kept her routine private for the most part, having personal devotions in her walk-in closet each morning where Darryl and I would hear her speaking in tongues through the wall. She had her routine, and I sat in front of the small TV in my bedroom and drowned hers out with mine.

I was in my tweens at this point and had begun struggling between my two identities warring for my soul. On one side were the stories I watched on TV and read in books, the allure of the fantastical and adventurous. On the other side was a deeply held belief in a battle between God and Satan, the real war that warned against entertainment as a tool of the devil to inculcate me into sin and lure me into the world and away from salvation.

The two were incompatible though, and led to a cognitive dissonance that became a secondary superpower to a kid who could do things like pointing out the Black-coded characters of a TV show. I learned to disassociate entertainment from my beliefs. The two sides couldn't occupy space in me at the same time. I lived a double life, where I was fully present when I was with pop culture, and when I was done, I would go back home to the house of God, back to *The Greatest Adventures: Stories from the Bible*, back to Derrick, Margo, and Moki, never to speak of the other side until it was their turn again.

Compartmentalizing my two identities allowed me to live without the debilitating fear of acknowledging that my soul was edging further away from God and towards Satan, and that in the ultimate battle of good versus evil, I was serving the latter. Separating them allowed me to enjoy both in their given times, like spending weekends with my dad and weekdays with my mom and loving them both.

There were only the occasional hiccups, like the crushing guilt that came during a Week of Prayer seminar. Or any sermon that ended with an altar call.

An altar call was when, after a particularly stirring sermon on the broader fight between God and Satan, good and evil, the Church versus the World, a pastor asked the Lord to send his Holy Spirit. A piano would play softly, and the pastor would tell a story.

He would say how there's someone out there, someone here tonight, who needs to hear this. That someone who needs to hear it knows that they've fallen by the wayside, that they've turned from God's word and they want to come back.

His eyes would be closed as he invited that person, with the help of the Holy Spirit, to have the strength to stand up. That while your feet are like bricks, while the Devil tries to hold onto your ankles, Satan's grasp would begin to shake at the strength of the Holy Spirit, if only you would stand up.

He would begin to preach louder.

And you would feel it, a tightness over your ankles. The weight on your body. He would claim the promises of Daniel 10:1 and Luke 9:1 saying, "Satan, I bind you away from this sanctuary. You will leave every man, woman, child, and infant alone as you go, and you go now."

You would feel that, too. You would feel everything, but while the piano played and the pastor spoke, you had yet to stand. That's when you would hear voices cry "amen," and notice that someone had stood. There would be a chorus of *Amens* in fact, and the person would be crying and there would be applause as that person walked to the altar.

The pastor would thank the Lord. He would say, "praise God." He would call them a sheep returning to the great shepherd's flock. He would proclaim them safe now. He would say that they are welcomed back, that they are loved.

Then he would hug them, and there would be a moment of pause, because he would know there are more. He would know the Holy Spirit isn't done. He would know, and you would, too.

I chose the altar. It spoke to my soul, to my desire to please others and feel the relief of a cosmic catharsis, and to shed the world's weight by giving myself to God. The demons, the confusion, the worry, and the fear could be laid at the foot of the cross. Everything would be okay. And I would be special. I would answer Sabbath altar calls, Week of Prayer altar calls, Sunday altar calls, a drive-by alter call…there wasn't an altar call or rebaptism opportunity I would pass. And in those moments, I never felt more redeemed. I gave myself to God, and his mercy washed over me.

PART TWO

"By beholding, we are to become changed; and as we meditate upon the perfections of the divine Model, we shall desire to become wholly transformed, and renewed in the image of His purity." - Ellen G. White

"How come he don't want me, man?" - Will Smith

CHAPTER 8

REAL CHRISTIANS

When I was 12 and my mom met Clifford Maycock, he struck me as someone who knew a lot about both Black people and the Bible. He wore a moustache, a toupee, and always a suit and tie. No matter the day of the week or the weather outside, Clifford, who went by Cliff, would wear a long-sleeved white shirt with a new tie. He was a Bible salesman and a lifelong Adventist, but he had also spent a season of his life outside the church in Black nightclubs in the '60s until he eventually gave his life back to Christ, and his crisp white shirts and black suits were a marriage of his former upscale nightlife and his renewed piety.

He helped my mom towards a reconciliation with the Seventh-day Adventist church. Her transition back to our original faith was never explained to Darryl and me, but one day she was speaking in tongues, one day she wasn't, and we were back to our Seventh-day Adventist ways, attending church on the Sabbath and reunited with our church family, all much to my grandma's relief. We had moved back to Detroit into a small three-bedroom bungalow at 6841 Rutland, on the west side of the city in a predominately Arab neighborhood on the border with Dearborn. It was the first house my mom ever bought, and we were proud of it. Darryl and I had our own rooms for the first time, though I often still slept in his out of habit and wanting to be close to him.

Cliff and my mom had begun dating before I realized what dating looked like, or understood that the man who was coming over to help fix broken chairs or mow our new lawn was in a growing relationship with her. He had begun to stay for dinner, and I enjoyed his presence for how self-assured he was, a confidence that gave his compliments extra power as he told Darryl and me how special we were, how we behaved so well, how we were so different from other boys he saw, disrespectful boys, immoral boys, worldly boys. His compliments were wrapped in criticisms of the types of people he hated, but I didn't notice or care as I absorbed his positive opinion of us. He was in his upper fifties, at least 15 years older than my mom, and he spoke like an amalgamation of Adventist piety mixed with jive talk from the 1970s, "Bring ye all the tithes into the storehouse" meets Clubber Lang from *Rocky III*.

He swooned over my mom. He swooned over Darryl and me. He wrapped my mom's hair in curlers in the evening, and when she thanked him, he said it was his life's honor, that he would do it every night, without fail, until the end of time. He used analogies to explain just how long eternity would be, and to explain both heaven and his undying adoration of my mother, the most beautiful, wonderful, intelligent, and classy woman he had ever met.

"Imagine a songbird flying down from the heavens and landing on a beautiful beach," he told us. "Imagine that bird picked up one grain of sand in its beak, and then flew back to the heavens. The bird came back once each year, picking up

86

a single grain of sand, and flying away, until the beach was completely empty of sand. All of that would be one moment," he would clap his hands just then, fast as lightning, "just one moment in the context of eternity. That's how long heaven will be, and that's how long I'll love your mother. We can't even imagine it."

He showered us with praise, love bombing us in a way I would recognize as the trait of a narcissist decades later, but for now, I was loved, and my mother was loved, and my brother was loved, and effortlessly so.

I hadn't gotten my parents back together with the blueprint laid by *The Parent Trap*, having failed to account for the fact that Darryl and I weren't separated twins, that my parents argued whenever they spoke, and that my mom was angry with my dad. I decided that my parents wouldn't get back together, but that if this new family was the alternative, I could be happy with that. It was still a family. My hope grew stronger when I learned that Cliff had a former family that he hated.

He had two children, an elementary school-aged son from his previous partner, and a daughter in her twenties from his first marriage. Cliff hated both his former partners. He described them as evil and detestable, who smoked and drank and did their best to keep his children from him so that they could raise them the wrong way without his interference. I learned the word "detest" by learning about his former partners, and his hatred of his previous families strengthened my confidence in ours, that we were a solid alternative to his other options, that our interests were aligned, that if he wanted a more perfect family as I did, he would find it in us.

His previous families came from when Cliff was a different person with a different name. He went by the name Yadao

Dorlin for a period of his life that he described as a time when he was "out in the world." What he meant was that he was living in sin, away from the Seventh-day Adventist church. He spoke about those years with shame mixed with a thinly veiled pride in his worldly exploits. To hear him tell it, his chief sin was that of Lucifer himself, a vanity in the wonder of his own being. He was beautiful. He spent his evenings in nightclubs. He danced wonderfully. To hear his stories was to imagine dance scenes from *Idlewild* or the opening of *Malcolm X*, live music and Lindy Hop dancers as Yadao Dorlin, the most beautiful among them, shoes shined perfect, hat tilted, clothes finely pressed, shone like a star.

He was a meticulous man, perhaps due to his strict upbringing by a stern father, but equally likely from his time in the army. He had lived many lives, from nightclub dancer to soldier to professional runner in the Michigan race circuit where he won countless medals. He told us how he would taunt other racers before the race, sometimes even jumping rope at the starting line before the race began, and then he would beat them. Every professional runner in Michigan hated him, and he loved it, because he knew they hated him for being better than them. Darryl and I thought he was exaggerating, but when we stumbled across a box of his trophies and medals when he moved in with us, they confirmed that his stories were true.

Clifford Maycock reverted to his original name after returning to the church though, and he eventually met my mother as Cliff instead of his flamboyant alter-ego, Yadao. He continued to wear only suits with a pressed white shirt, along with an accent piece to highlight his inner self such as a white shirt with pinstripes instead of a plain white one, or a pure white handkerchief in his suit jacket pocket, or black shoes shined long enough that you could see your reflection.

Despite tales of his flamboyancy, though, my brother and I never saw him as particularly stylish. To a twelve-year-old and fifteen-year-old, the suits only accentuated what was a gravely serious look he kept on his face when he spoke about the things he hated, sin and the consequences of it. Those consequences were all around us in the pain and poverty of Detroit, all from the meat-eating, God-rejecting, ignorantly sinful people around us. When Cliff started driving us to school, the black suits and grave expressions started to embarrass us right away.

"Uh, your dad looks like a mortician," one of Darryl's friends said, as Cliff came to pick us up from school one day.

"Step-dad," Darryl said, distancing himself from the new man in our lives.

His friend wasn't wrong. Cliff wore a scowl on his face and he had a propensity to debate fiercely with non-Seventh-day Adventist "so-called Christians," which made Darryl worried about ever having him around school. His high school friends were old enough to recognize Cliff's oddity and make fun of it, and make fun of Darryl by extension, so Darryl began opting to walk home from school or catch rides with other families. I was too young to be embarrassed, though. All I saw was Cliff's passion when he spoke, the way he would come alive in a debate. He approached a debate with the same confidence he approached a race, knowing he would win the competition. He was stronger, faster, and smarter. And he had the facts on his side.

His passion for the Seventh-day Adventist health message bled over to my mom as he pushed her to ban meat from the house and insisted that we all be vegetarians. There were rules about proper diet and health. Some were unofficial, like being vegetarian. Others were official, as spelled out in the Bible or Seventh-day Adventist manual that outlined our church's stance on abstaining from pork, shrimp, and other unclean food by the standards of Leviticus. Where pious Adventists sacrificed eating meat altogether, others who weren't ready to make the leap could at least limit themselves to "clean" animals that met certain standards, like having split hooves. Pork was out of the question, as well as scavengers. We were meant to be "real Christians," and so our mom acquiesced. Darryl and I became vegetarians, me at twelve years old and Darryl at fifteen.

Artificial meat helped ease my transition, with companies like Worthington and Morning Star Farms producing countless substitutes that I had grown up eating in the Seventh-day Adventist church, and I ate them so often that to me they tasted better than real meat. "Veggie Links," "Stripples," and "Grillers" were the names we used for sausage, bacon, and burgers. I once made the mistake of sharing Grillers with a non-Adventist friend without realizing that fake meat was one of the areas of Adventism to be selective about sharing. It had become so common to me that I began to think it was normal, a delusion that was short lived as he took a bite and spat it out.

I was taught that the health message was an entry point to teach my beliefs to others, and that visitors to our church would notice when they would stay for potluck after worship service on the Sabbath. While talk of heaven and hell could persuade a potential convert to close the door and harden their hearts, talking about healthy living could open the door for a conversation that could lead to an invitation to God.

Occasionally a well-intentioned visitor would plan to bring food as a polite gesture for being invited to church, leading to rumors among us kids in Sabbath School that someone had brought chicken to potluck.

"It's Sam's chicken," someone insisted, referring to a specific Midwestern Adventist replacement for real chicken, made with soy and fried in breading. I loved Sam's chicken and could binge until my stomach hurt.

"No, they brought chicken-chicken," one of the kids said in their "you-in-trouble" voice.

Some of us thought it was hilarious, the mere idea of someone bringing real chicken to a church potluck being funny and salacious. Most of us were raised Adventist, and some of them had been vegetarians their whole lives. Other kids hoped that it was true, having *not* been raised lifelong vegetarian Adventists, who knew what real chicken tasted like and hoped they'd be saved from vegetarian meat that day.

Adults, on the other hand, found neither humor nor optimism in the rumor. On hearing the news, one church elder scrunched his face in doubt.

"Who told you that?" he asked.

Another, an older Jamaican woman furrowed her brow in anger, "Where'dye say you saw the chicken?" her accent heaviest when her emotions stirred. "You sure it's not the Sam's chicken, boy?"

As it turned out, someone actually had brought real meat to the church potluck in the form of meatloaf, and I eavesdropped as the adults in the kitchen decided what to do. They debated various options, the most important question being whether they could serve the meat at all. Finally, they came to a compromise. They would serve the meat from the kitchen, away from the rest of the food on the serving tables in the recreation room, to anyone who specifically requested it. It would also be an opportunity to witness to our new guests if they asked about their contribution, thereby turning the debacle into a blessing.

I learned the extent I could be valued for abstentions and sacrifices. I would hope to abstain from meat, alcohol, drugs, and sex. Martyrdom was almost a dream, the ultimate sacrifice after being taught that our church would be persecuted for our beliefs in the last days, and that a tyrannical government would keep us from worshipping on the Sabbath. I learned two important events that were predicted to come, The Second Coming of Christ, and the Sunday Blue Law that would precede it.

The Sunday Blue Law would be the last sign of the End Times before Jesus' Second Coming, and the End Times meant torture and persecution for true believers. Many of us would be thrown in jail. Some would fold, but the faithful among us would pass God's test, stand firm to our beliefs, and be persecuted. Soon the world would fall into complete chaos. In the very end all would be lost, and the world would be in peril without God. We would leave the cities and move to the countryside, living off the land. Many of us would be captured, questioned, and asked to renounce our faith, and resistance would mean the risk of being killed.

My childhood imagination pictured a post-Apocalyptic military state, with myself, my brother, and my friends from church tied to wooden posts lined in a row. I would recall stories of those who faced death and were saved by God's intervention. My favorite hymns, "It Is Well with My Soul" and "Midnight Cry" captured the beauty of that moment as an amalgamation of Bible stories and animated fantasies from the cartoons and comic book panels that were my secret sins. Gospel versions of "It Is Well with My Soul" and "Midnight Cry" played like a film, a 3-arc story with preparation and faithfulness, action and betrayal, survival and fear and salvation that built to their climax at the choir's crescendo. They were the perfect songs to capture that glory, validation, and vindication in all the trials I would face in life and the sacrifices I made. It would all be worth it in that moment. Every tribulation, challenge, and tear led there. It wouldn't be the anguished cry of my grandma in the night, but the exact opposite, the joy of Christ's return.

My favorite stories were the ones I heard about captives standing for God despite facing their death. The best parables came from someone standing tall for the Lord. I saw a love for persecution and self-reliance, paired with fantasies of martyrdom, following in Jesus' footsteps and fulfilling the prophesies that would lead to his return. In the stories, sometimes the challenges were a test and the Lord protected them, like in the story of Job from the Bible.

Job was a pious man who loved the Lord and lived a perfect life. He was virtually sinless and adherent to God's will. One day, as the story goes, Satan told the Lord that the only reason Job was so faithful was because his life was going so well.

"Look at him," I imagine Satan to have said, "He has a wonderful wife, beautiful kids, and lots of money. Why wouldn't he worship you?" But God wasn't buying it, so Satan continued. "How you think somebody's loyal who hasn't been tested?"

Then God, goaded by Satan, went to prove Satan wrong. God took everything from Job. He killed Job's wife. He killed his kids. He took away his money. Yet Job continued praying.

Job stayed faithful.

After proving his point, God rewarded Job by giving him a new wife, kids, and riches. Job passed the test as an eternal example of unwavering faith.

Job's story reminded me of a hymn we sang at church, "Trust and Obey," with a chorus that sang "trust and obey, for there's no other way, to be happy in Jesus, than to trust and obey." To claim an unwavering faith in God was cheap. To prove faithfulness, I had to sacrifice.

Other stories featured heroes who looked death in the eye for their beliefs and chose to die for God. Standing for God was a win-win, either you live after proving your dedication in the face of your oppressors, or you die in the ultimate test of faith and inherit the greatest rewards in the kingdom of heaven. Either way, to face martyrdom was both an earthly and spiritual do-or-die moment.

The story of Shadrach, Meeshach, and Abednego was among my favorites. Babylon's King Nebuchadnezzar had gone wild with power and had a statue built in his own image. His statue was based on a dream, where he had imagined a head made of gold, chest and arms made of silver, a torso of bronze, legs made of iron, and feet made of both iron and clay. The prophet Daniel interpreted the king's dream, which was something none of Nebuchadnezzar's chief magicians and counselors had been able to do. The statue represented the empires that would follow Nebuchadnezzar's rule, from their Babylonian empire as the head of gold to the subsequent Medo-Persian chest and arms, to its Greek torso, to its Roman legs. Its feet, made of a mix of iron and clay, represented my own dad's greatest fear, the unification of the church and state into a one-world government that would lead to the apocalypse. At the end of Nebuchadnezzar's dream, Daniel interpreted, was a large stone that crashed into the statue's feet, representing God's destruction of it all.

When Nebuchadnezzar's statue was built, he scheduled

a kingdom-wide gathering for the statue's unveiling.

"When the gong sounds," he said, "everyone will bow to me at the same time," he commanded. "It'll be fabulous." The King also had a fierce temper and knew the whole thing would be ruined if people didn't bow right, so he made a decree. "Anyone who does not bow when the beat drops will be thrown into this fiery furnace."

Daniel had three friends though, Shadrach, Meshach, and Abednego, who knew God had commanded against bowing to idols. "You shall not make for yourself an image in the form of anything in heaven above or on the earth beneath or in the waters below," the Second Commandment says. It continues, "You shall not bow down to them or worship them, for I, the Lord your God, am a jealous God, punishing the children for the sin of the parents to the third and fourth generation of those who hate me, but showing love to a thousand genera-tions of those who love me and keep my commandments."

Shadrach, Meshach, and Abednego had the quintessen-tial persecution predicament. Did they kneel before the statue of King Nebuchadnezzar and save their lives, or did they stand defiant, and pray for God's protection?

I imagined they at least had to discuss their options. Maybe Meshach was like, "I think God might understand. He wouldn't want us to be burned alive."

"You're right," Shadrach added. "We're more useful to him alive than dead. I mean, imagine how many people we can convert if we stay living."

Abednego may have reasoned they should bow now and repent later. "Sometimes it's better to ask forgiveness than be burned alive in a furnace, as they say."

When the gong sounded, everyone bowed on their knees, their faces into the ground. All but Shadrach, Meshach, and

Abednego.

"This is a disaster," King Nebuchadnezzar would have screamed. "Who are those three?" Royal advisors told the King their names and why they would not bow, for it was against their beliefs to bow before anyone but God. King Nebuchadnezzar summoned the three to be brought before him. "You are ruining this party." he told them. "I'll give you one last chance. Bow to the statue, or I swear I will throw you into that furnace."

The three looked at one another.

"I'll do it, I'm not playing around here," King Nebuchadnezzar yelled.

Shadrach, Meshach, and Abednego had come so far in their stance for God that they couldn't turn around now. They wouldn't. King Nebuchadnezzar was pissed, and ordered the furnace's temperature to be raised ten times hotter before demanding the boys be thrown in.

"It's been real," Abednego said. "See you on the other side." Bone Thugz N Harmony's "Crossroads" began to play as they were chaperoned to the furnace and shoved inside. But amazingly, something happened.

"Were there not three boys I sent to the furnace?" asked Nebuchadnezzar to his royal advisors. "Because within the flames, I see four."

And it true, there was a fourth in the flames. It was an angel sent from God, protecting Shadrach, Meshach, and Abednego from harm. King Nebuchadnezzar was so impressed by the Lord he ordered the boys pulled from the fire and invited them to his table in another example of God holding it down for the loyal.

There are a million more such stories. Daniel and the Lions' Den was the same premise, only replace a furnace with a den of hungry lions. My mind was full of inspiring stories.

Along with Bible stories, we learned modern parables as well. My favorite was taught to me by a church elder in Sabbath School who was preparing us to be strong for God. In the last days, we Christians would hide in a bunker where we would have stores of food and water to last for months. We would spend our time praying, studying, and waiting for the Second Coming. An armed man would find the entrance to the bunker and call over his friends to pry it open. They would pull open the door to reveal the cave beneath where we hid. After climbing down, they would point their guns at us and offer us mercy.

"Anyone who doesn't believe is free to go," they would say. "The rest of you can stay and be killed." After a short pause, one person would get up and leave. Another person would follow suit, and another. Soon half the room would be gone, save for a loyal few who remained behind to die.

"Good," the armed man said, lowering his weapon. "I wanted to be with real Christians."

CHAPTER 9

AVALON

Several months after we had become vegetarians, I learned that Darryl really wasn't. Being more rebellious against our new lifestyle, he had secretly continued eating meat outside our house, so much that his friends laughed hysterically when I naively turned down meat after school one day by mentioning we were vegetarians.

"Darryl?" they laughed. "A vegetarian? He eats more meat than any of us. He literally just had a pepperoni pizza today." I was embarrassed by them knowing more about my brother than I did, but the information hurt, too. We had been in this struggle together, only he was leaving me behind to eat meat on his own like a cellmate smuggling food each day and leaving you to starve. I worried that the chasm between us was growing by nature of our age difference, three years apart, at an age where such a gap feels significant. He was in high school now, and he was popular, talking to girls, and eating meat. The hurt was eclipsed only by the fear that my brother was being lost to "the world," not only by eating meat, but pork. I had eaten pork only twice in my life, once when a neighbor made bacon and had made fun of me for never having tasted it, and again when my junior high school cafeteria served ham and I was curious enough to pray for God to bless it before trying a small corner. Pork was on the worse side of things we knew to avoid, along with shellfish and caffeine.

If the chasm between Darryl and I was growing, it would soon close as Cliff grew more comfortable asserting his role in our home. It began with minor criticisms, as Darryl and I began to be scolded for any number of infractions. They ranged from creasing a check because paper needed to remain crisp and we needed to learn to respect money, to wasting water while washing dishes because you're meant to plug the sink and use that water for soaking and washing and only use fresh water for rinsing, and we boys need to learn to respect money, to improperly cutting tomatoes because you don't chop off the top but carve around the stem, which we would learn if we bought our own food and stopped wasting money.

The more imposing Cliff grew, the more Darryl and I became closer because of it. When Cliff would criticize us, he would lecture us with stories of how his own father would beat him for entering his bedroom because children weren't allowed in their parent's bedrooms, or for Cliff taking off the undershirt that he found itchy because his father demanded that he wear an undershirt. He kept us in line with lectures that could last hours, sometimes days, on a single, pedantic topic, like how you should refill an ice tray each time you used it to keep it full instead of waiting until it was empty, or how sleeping in after the sunrise makes you lazy, or how mismanagement of your time is a sin. He had incredible endurance and took pride in proving himself right and others wrong. At first, his criticisms made us feel bad, but it wasn't long before

Darryl and I began to laugh about them behind his back, sometimes making eye contact during his lectures themselves and cracking a smile or choking back a laugh, which only made him more upset, which only made us want to laugh more.

That summer Cliff decided to teach Darryl and me discipline by forcing us awake that at 7 a.m. to run with him. Darryl's best friend, Deshawn, lived only a mile away but spent most summer nights at our house, so Deshawn was made to run, too. We would collectively fake sick when possible, but more often than not we were scolded into a car and driven to River Rouge Park where we would run.

Darryl got the worst of it by being the only one athletic enough to keep up with Cliff on six-mile runs, meaning he had to spend over an hour with Cliff each day during warm-ups, runs, stretches, and cooldowns. But each run would begin the same for Deshawn and me, as we would start to run just behind Darryl and Cliff until the first major curve where the trees would obstruct the line of sight between us and them and we could stop running. Then Deshawn and I would walk the rest of the way, cutting through the park and walking two miles in the time it took Cliff and Darryl to run six. When the car was back in sight at the end of our loop around the park and Cliff and Darryl stood waiting for us to finish, Deshawn and I would begin running again as if we had never stopped, sprinting to the finish. If Darryl was frustrated by us falling behind, he never showed it. His runs with Cliff seemed to be something else to him than they were to Deshawn and me. He would keep up with Cliff to show that he could.

Signs started to show that Cliff's moral convictions lived distant from his actions. One arose when it turned out that Cliff hadn't been legally divorced from his previous wife before marrying my mom in the Seventh-day Adventist church. I couldn't understand the legal details, or why Cliff said he was being targeted, or what "disfellowship" meant, but I did understand that Cliff was angry and that there would be some sort of trial. I sat in the pews at the Northwest Seventh-day Adventist Church as board members heard the case against my mom and Cliff from the pastor who wanted to end their membership to the church that I had been raised in. I thought that losing the trial meant that they couldn't be together, and that I would lose the new semblance of family I had only just gotten. I wanted Cliff to stay. I wanted to hold onto what we had, even if that meant summer runs and angry lectures.

Cliff wanted to leave before the church board gave their verdict, and we prayed together in our living room when we got home. We got the phone call from a church friend a few minutes later. We had won by one vote. I was relieved.

At the same time, I started watching *Gargoyles*. "One thousand years ago, superstition and the sword ruled," and I was given one of the most thoughtful series I had ever seen. And while it might seem on the surface that it was a regular action cartoon series, *Gargoyles* proved itself in each episode as a program with a message that was simple, yet profound in its rarity among its peers. It took off the kid gloves, put both hands on your shoulders, and said, "You're old enough to handle this."

The story followed an intelligent, nocturnal species called gargoyles that turned into stone during the day and awakened at night. Their bond with humans was one of protection, where they lived alongside us safeguarding ancient castles and families for hundreds of years, until they were betrayed by humans in 994 AD and frozen in stone by a magic spell that would only break when their castle "rises above the clouds."

Everyone in their clan was murdered except five gargoyles who weren't destroyed, and who awoke in modern-day New York City, the last of their kind.

That was already heavy for a child, but *Gargoyles* was only just getting started. Not for shock or awe, though, but because this series had a few things to say. It rolled the dice and made the gamble. *Gargoyles* would discuss mature themes using complex story arcs, all hidden in the guise of an action cartoon, and it would trust kids to get it.

When a battle-scarred Demona turned Manhattan to stone and started crumbling bodies down 5th Avenue? People died, yo. Nine people, on a kids' show. Demona saw a woman carrying shopping bags and said, "Here, let me help you with those packages," *And shot her with the cannon. She blew her arms off, fam.* A couple was turned to stone nearby, and she blasted them, too. *And laughed.* Demona quoted Latin spells that reminded me of my mom speaking in tongues:

Omnes conspecti, omnes auditi,
In nocte usque ad saxum commutate
Dum calum ardeat

The first time I realized *Gargoyles* was different was in one of the earliest episodes when one gargoyle, Broadway, accidentally shot his friend Elisa and nearly ended her life. The small pool of blood under Elisa, the fact it was later censored from TV, his emotion that followed, and his lasting hatred of guns, all showed that this wasn't a regular show.

The person who raised their castle above the clouds to bring the gargoyles back to life was David Xanatos, my earliest introductions to complex villains, one for whom "villain" is perhaps too thin a word to accurately describe him.

In a decade of Dr. Robotniks, Queen Beryls, and Shredders, David Xanatos was an antagonist whose motivations evolved and whose character changed over the entire series. He often did terrible things in the name of profit or science, while at other times he showed the character of a hero. Watching David Xanatos was the first time I learned to judge actions outside of a character label, because watching him forced me to think about his actions separately from his reputation. "Good" people weren't always right, and "evil" people weren't always wrong.

A skilled strategist, scientist, and businessman, Xanatos was unlike most villains I had ever seen before. He wasn't on a singular quest for world domination because he already had wealth. He thought revenge was foolish. He saw emotion as distracting and he valued logic over all, yet he would still do anything to protect his family.

I wanted to think like him, I wanted to be as clever as him. I pictured myself wearing a dark jacket and a ponytail when I came up with pre-adolescent schemes and learned to play chess because Xanatos played. While being the "bad guy," David Xanatos charmed me with his intellectual curiosity.

No character has ever taught me a love of learning as much as Xanatos, because man, he made it look so badass. So unique was his character that there's a TV trope in his honor, the "Xanatos Gambit," referring to his ability to make any situation work out in his favor, whether it went according to plan or not. A Xanatos Gambit is a plan for which all foreseeable outcomes benefit the mastermind creator, including ones that superficially appear to be failure. You fight me, I kill you, I win. You fight me, you kill me, the people demonize you, I still win. He reminded me of Cliff, who boasted that he could win whatever argument he was in, that he always had the facts, and that he could prove it. There was no such thing as losing with Xanatos, no such thing as failure. There just "was," and what "was" would always serve his goals.

Antagonist aside, *Gargoyles* forced me into maturity by challenging me with complex plots and moral quandaries. The show introduced Shakespearean drama quite literally, with Macbeth as an integral and ongoing character. It wasn't a character named after Macbeth, it was Shakespeare's actual Macbeth, spiritually tied to the tragic life of Demona after she lost her lover, her family, her culture, and her faith.

Macbeth and Demona were bound together throughout history for centuries. Unexpectedly, it would be a story arc called "Avalon" that would resonate with me the most, well after *Gargoyles* ended.

In the Avalon episodes, four characters, Elisa, Goliath, his daughter Angela, and their gargoyle-dog Bronx traveled on a canoe through a foggy sea that led them to strange new lands. The premise behind Avalon was that it was a magical place on earth, and that it was hidden from every map. Instead of taking you where you wanted to go, Avalon took its lost travelers where it felt they needed to be, and it was up to them to find meaning in why they were there. In each episode, the four would dock their boat and be strangers in a strange land. They would have to find their purpose, adapt, survive, and leave when they were done, having changed that place in some way, or changed themselves as they got back on their small boat and rowed back into the fog. I would travel on a similar journey soon, though I didn't know it yet.

I also didn't know at first how much its themes of racism and xenophobia would help me feel less alone. Craftily woven throughout the series, tolerance, courage, and integrity were taught simultaneously through the stories of the humans' relationships with the gargoyles, and more subtly through Elisa and Goliath themselves. They were the two Black characters I wanted so badly to become lovers but thought that they couldn't, that they wouldn't, that children's television wouldn't allow it, that they would never be lovers. Until they were. Until they did.

Salli Richardson-Whitfield was the voice of Elisa Maza, and Elisa was perfect to me in every way. My first crush, Elisa, had a Black mother and a Native American father and was one of the few Black women leads I could find growing up. She was smart, charming, loyal, tough, and funny. She was a dynamic character who stood out as the moral compass of the show, even when I thought that job belonged to Goliath. Elisa was as close to a perfectly written character as I could imagine, and she was a Black woman.

Opposite Elisa was the star of the show and leader of the clan, Goliath, voiced by Keith David, a Black actor with the voice of God. Keith David gave life to a character whose appearance struck fear in others, but whose masculinity lived in his emotion, his vulnerability, and his struggles. Goliath's journey was one in search of love and acceptance after betrayal and pain. Goliath was lost in place and time, and then lost in the mysteries of Avalon, yet he accepted that it would always be a journey and a struggle, and that the best way forward was with bravery and trust for those you loved. It didn't always work out and Goliath was dealt terrible emotional pain, but he would keep pressing forward.

Race, betrayal, trust...*Gargoyles* challenged me more than any other network cartoon dared try, and it was the most entertaining cartoon on television that challenged me without talking down to me. *Gargoyles* trusted me with matters that were above my age. *Gargoyles* gave me a Black couple in an animated series and made me find hope despite their challenges. *Gargoyles* had a message and told me I was mature enough to handle it. And so, I was.

My mom wasn't speaking in tongues anymore, but she was still in conversation with God. One morning, she heard the voice of the Holy Spirit who told her that weekends weren't enough, that I needed a Seventh-day Adventist education so I could be raised with the proper direction of God's one true church. I was still half asleep when she told me that morning, and it hit me like a brick.

The school year had already started though, and I was one month into eighth grade homeroom at Detroit Urban Lutheran School, the same school I had attended for over seven years, the school where I had learned from Ms. Nelson, Ms. Henry, Ms. Prue, Ms. Anderson, Mr. Hughes, Ms. Winston, Mr. Grant, and now Ms. Patterson. All my friends were there. My childhood was there. Darryl was there, attending the high school expansion of the school that I naturally thought I would attend as well. I tried to convince my mom of these things as I started to cry. But mom had already decided with the help of Cliff and the Holy Spirit that Seventh-day Adventist education couldn't wait another day. Darryl was in his junior year of high school and old enough to be exempt, but I could still be saved.

That morning I wasn't taken to the school I'd gone to for the past seven years, but instead the car pulled into a quiet lot off a country road with a one-story white-brick school on the left and a matching church on the right. It happened that fast.

This was Plymouth, Michigan, a more distant suburb of Detroit than the Southfield suburb where we had previously lived. Where Southfield felt like a hood rich version of Detroit, Plymouth was where urban Michigan transitioned closer to *rural* Michigan. White Michigan. *Very* white Michigan.

When we arrived, I sat crying in the back seat.

Sobbing quietly was hard work, and the more I realized how bad I was at it, the more frustrated I became. Suppressing the cry only led to more snot, and to the shallow breathing and rapid tremble of the bottom lip that comes with "manly" tears, the ability to cry without the benefit of actual cathartic release.

A small sign stood on a well-manicured plot of grass in front of the school that read "Metropolitan Seventh-day Adventist Junior Academy." It wasn't enough to be a mouthful I thought, it had to have a subscript as well, something about preparing its students for the kingdom of heaven. I rolled my eyes, my anger redirecting towards the faith I had been raised in, and towards the God who had led my mom to her decision. But then the thought of involuntarily asking God for forgiveness came into my mind. Asking God's forgiveness was something of a reflex, a quiet pact between me and God to atone for sins unseen.

The car came to a stop in front of the main doors and the engine turned silent. I saw my mom in my peripheral vision trying to make empathetic eye contact through the rear-view mirror. Her eye contact said, "I'm doing this because I love you," and asked for a semblance of understanding. I didn't want to give her the satisfaction.

Averting my eyes led me to look through the long row of windows lining the school, each a different classroom. There were four rooms with two large windows each. I slouched down and sniffled soft enough to hide the sound but hard enough to keep the stream of snot from reaching my mouth. I tasted snot and salt anyway and commanded myself not to swallow until I had a chance to go to a bathroom and spit in the sink.

"Hi," said a stout, round white woman who pleasantly greeted us on our entrance through the front glass doors. "I'm Mary Simon. Welcome to Metropolitan SDA Academy. I'm so glad to meet you."

As much as I wanted to shrink behind my mother, I refused to look cowardly as she exchanged pleasantries with Mrs. Simon. "And you must be Jordan!" Mrs. Simon extended her hand, and I shook it weakly. Her hands were soft, and her kind enthusiasm made it easier for me to brave her eye contact. "We're so happy to have you here. Would you like to take a quick tour? We're a small school, but we like to think of it instead as a big family."

I imagined myself yelling to her that she was no family of mine, this white woman in a place I've never been to and where I didn't want to be, but her voice brought me a degree of comfort as we started down the single hallway that held entrances to each classroom. There were four of them, all neat with rows of tables, two chairs to each. *How can a school have four classrooms?* I thought.

I began to convince myself that this was just a phase. I would only need to survive it for a short while, and my mom would come to her senses and things would go back to normal. I'd be back at Detroit Urban, back with my friends, back to cartoons on weekdays and God on weekends. All I had to do was dislike this place enough. If given the option to sink or swim, I would voluntarily close my eyes and take in water, and she would have no choice but to throw a raft and bring me back. It wouldn't be difficult, it wouldn't even be dishonest. I would never love this place, this white Adventist school that broke the treaty that separated the factions of my life.

Keeping a wounded look on my face would help do the trick, so as Mrs. Simon explained the bell schedule and afterschool activities I was sure to offset mom's courteous interest by showing a complete lack of my own.

"Is this our new student?" asked a smiling, young white woman. She introduced herself as Ms. Samborski, the home-room teacher for eighth and ninth grades, and I pieced together the next oddity of my setting, that the school had so few students that each teacher presided over at least two grades at a time. Multiple grades shared a single classroom with about eight or nine students in each grade. None of this felt like a real school. I hated it. And I hated my mom for bringing me there, for pulling me out of school on a random day and rearranging my whole life as if I were one of the bad kids who needed a little extra Jesus to be saved.

I felt that my mom had weaponized the Bible against me. "Seek ye first the kingdom of God" was one of the many verses learned from years of regularly attending church, and now it taunted me as an inscription in a sign for this school that was ruining my life. My mom had echoed its sentiment that morning when she explained her newfound dedication to Seventh-day Adventist education.

"Seek ye first the kingdom of God and his righteousness, and all these things shall be added unto you," my mom quoted.

Please don't say the *hallelujah* part, I thought to myself. Don't say it.

"...*hallelujah*."

I was in hell.

"This is Jordan and his mother, Ms. Calhoun," Mrs. Simon said as she introduced us to Ms. Samborski.

"Mrs. Maycock," mom corrected, using her newly married name. It made me wince. I was still adjusting to the change, and Cliff had begun to treat Darryl and me a little differently after he married my mom. Where he had incessantly praised us before, he'd begun to criticize, and I wondered how much of his influence led to my new situation. We were evolving from a Sabbath-keeping family to one that was vegetarian, went to church every Sabbath and prayer meetings on Wednesdays, had family devotions every night of the week, and had now sent their kid to a Seventh-day Adventist school.

"What's your favorite subject?" Ms. Samborski asked.

I didn't want to encourage conversation. I wanted to name a subject that didn't lend itself to follow-up questions. Social studies would be off limits. English would be a risk. Stick to the strategy, give a cold, one-word answer, and have some self-respect.

"Algebra," I decided.

"That's great!" *Why is that great?* "I'm the Algebra teacher." *Of course, you are.* "Let me show you around the classroom." *This backfired.*

Shit, I thought plainly, then looked down and apologized in my heart, asking forgiveness for cursing. Mom, Mrs. Simon, and Ms. Samborski couldn't hear my thoughts, but God did.

I remembered that I had yet to spit or swallow since tasting my own snot back in the car.

"Can I go to the bathroom?" I asked.

"Of course, sweetheart." Mom put her arm over my shoulder as I pulled away. "Where's the bathroom?" she asked Mrs. Simon.

"It's right at the end of the hall, on your left. Last door there before the end." Mrs. Simon said.

I broke away, and for the first time I walked the length of the school that was to be my home for the next year or, in teenage perspective, forever.

I passed the urinals and looked for feet hiding under

the stalls as casually as possible. I wanted to make sure I was alone, but that could backfire if someone noticed me hunched over to look under doors, or if I made eye-contact with some unwitting squatter through the crack between the door of the bathroom stall.

I washed out my mouth and left the water running as I looked up in the bathroom mirror. And then I heard the door swing open from around the corner as a white boy my age walked in wearing a backwards hat.

"Yo," he said as he offered to give me dap. "I'm Kyle. You listen to DMX?"

CHAPTER 10

FIGHT LIKE A [BLACK] GIRL

There were two other Black students from the city who attended Metropolitan Seventh-day Adventist Junior Academy, or "Metro" for short. Their names were Brandi and Precious, two sisters I had known since childhood. They attended Northwest Seventh-day Adventist church, the one I grew up in, where I served in the Pathfinders and earned the patch that my grandma would sew over with brown thread. Brandi and Precious lived only a few miles away from me but had attended Metro for years, so on top of being my carpool ride as their mom, Claudette, picked me up every morning to commute from Detroit to the suburbs, when we arrived at school, they were also my tour guides as to who's who and what's what.

They would tell me who was popular, and why. They would tell me why girls named Kirsten, Shelly, and Emma were best friends, where they shopped for their clothes, where they lived, and what their parents did. It was foreign to me, I had never spent time with white kids my age, but Brandi and Precious had been toggling between the Black neighborhood where we lived and the white suburb where we were in school for years.

Brandi was my age, having just become a teenager, and Precious was two or three years younger. I was grateful to them both for existing, for explaining that, yes, the white kids' jokes were corny, or yes, their parents still do make their lunches, or no, making better and faster insults isn't social currency here because the white kids will just call you mean. I was familiar with all the Adventist quirks, like many of them being vegetarian and having "Bible" class, but learning white culture was its own education. Brandi and Precious had become a touchstone for my sanity, my Darryl away from Darryl, two people who walked where I walked, saw what I saw, and felt it was weird, whether we talked about it aloud or not. Sometimes a glance was enough. When I would get home to explain "white school" to Darryl, it was Brandi and Precious whose explanations I would quote to him like trying to teach a math equation that I didn't quite understand myself.

But while I was thankful to Brandi and Precious for sharing my experience, I was embarrassed for their mom. She took me to school every morning and drove me back home, a relationship that inherently turned Claudette into my surrogate mother and made Brandi and Precious my sisters, the three of us a small family on the seas of Avalon. But I was embarrassed because Claudette was also the school janitor.

Claudette worked at Metro to help afford sending Brandi and Precious there, and the job offered the added benefit of discounted tuition for her daughters. Our leaving school at the end of the day meant finishing cleaning it first, and I was deputized alongside Brandi and Precious to help clean. The sooner we finished, the sooner we would get home, so we worked together. Every day after last period we would get started, vacuuming the classrooms, cleaning the chalkboards, squeegeeing the windows, wiping the toilets, mopping the bathrooms, and taking out the trash. I liked the teamwork, the race to clean faster, better, and smarter to maximize the free time I would have at home to watch TV and talk with Darryl. But I hated it, too. I was a kid and being the family who cleaned up after white people felt like a constant reminder of our place.

I felt angry when they would spill glitter on the floor or miss the trash can. Sometimes they would retort that the janitor would clean it up, knowing full well who the janitors were, but leaving the rest as subtext. I came to recognize what white meanness looked like, and the form it took that was different from when I would play the Dozens game with my friends at Detroit Urban. White meanness wasn't direct. It lived under a veil of subtlety or deniability. Sometimes their meanness could even come in the form of niceness, an errant "I'm impressed" at something unimpressive, or "that's so nice, I didn't know you have that where you live." I was embarrassed that at the end of the day they were right, that we *would* clean it all up.

Every day when I heard the roar of the vacuum down the hall after the final bell, I started to feel embarrassed, and I would feel that way until we cleaned the last messes and emptied the final trash cans and got in the car and out of sight of white people. But Brandi and Precious didn't seem embarrassed. They seemed above it, unfazed. It seemed that Brandi and Precious were miles ahead of me in not caring what white people thought.

Whatever my experience, I could only imagine what it was like for Brandi, Precious, and Claudette.

If I had it bad with onscreen representation, Brandi and

Precious had it worse. White girls had endless options. Black girls had Lisa Turtle or Jodie Landon.

Aside from scarce depictions of Black girl leads in animation, television, and movies, a growing trend of teen dance movies like *Save the Last Dance* would show Black culture as most valuable when mastered by white people, especially white women. They could take from Black culture what was popular and add the credibility that cultural dominance affords. White women could have a foot in both worlds and have both feet adored. Brandi and Precious had *The Proud Family* and *Bring It On* on the horizon, but cross-cultural hip hop romances starring thin white women would spur scenes from *Stomp the Yard*, *Step Up*, *Honey*, *Street Dance*, and *Bring It On: All or Nothing*. Brandi and Precious would need to be prepared to survive an irresistible formula from moviemakers built on a particularly insidious bait and switch, where pop culture had taught us to root for the underdog and then wrote the underdogs as white women.

Meanwhile, I was watching movies like *Rookie of the Year*, *The Mighty Ducks*, and *Angels in the Outfield*. They were all about rag-tag teams who pulled it together to overcome their athletic bullies. They lived in the wake of the cinematic success of the Rocky franchise that led to decades of cheering for the modest underdog against the dominant, often dishonest champion. To be favored to win was virtually synonymous with being the bad guy, as kids' sports villains skipped the Apollo Creed antagonists and went straight to the Clubber Langs and Ivan Dragos. Every *Karate Kid* had its cheap-hitting Johnny Lawrence, with few exceptions.

It was the decade of the sports outcast, where nerds learned to skate, the uncoordinated learned to run, the losers learned to win. It set the perfect stage for women in sports.

Revolutionary women. Fearless women. White women. I loved one more than all the rest, and her name was Ice Box.

In the opening scene of Warner Brothers' *Little Giants*, a young Ed O'Neill played the archetypical tough coach who was running his team into the ground, yelling for them to run faster, to work harder, to show him something.

"Dig, dig, dig...Come on, gentlemen, suck it up," he yelled.

After a hard collision on the field, a huddle of little league football players circled around a boy whose body had been given back to the earth after taking a shoulder pad to his gut. His short, abrupt scream was cut off before it even had a chance to live a full life.

"Oh, baby, now we're talking," coach yelled.

The tackler took off her helmet and it was Ice Box, this cold-blooded assassin, dirt on her face like a Dalmatian trying to escape Cruella de Vil. Ice Box was the coach's niece, rough enough to tumble with the boys as the iconic tomboy of 1994. She also had the greatest nickname of all time in lieu of her real name, Becky.

When it came time for the pee-wee football team to select its players, though, no amount of talent or family bond could save her from being cut from tryouts. You could almost see the five stages of grief play out over the young girl's face as players were called to pick up their jerseys and she realized her name wouldn't be called. And the team coach made it clear the reason Ice Box couldn't play football on his team.

"I hate to break it to ya, but Ice Box is a girl," coach told his brother, Becky's single father. To add weight to the gender role soon to be shattered, he added "Maybe if you start treating her like a girl, she'd start acting like one."

"Like a girl" was a common phrase, an insult that didn't

need meaner add-ons or further explanation. To do something like a girl was to do something inferior because girls *are* inferior. Run like a girl, catch like a girl, throw like a girl, fight like a girl, anything you did like a girl was the opposite of doing it right, like a man.

Ice Box and the other ragamuffins, all cut from the little league Dallas Cowboys, formed the Little Giants, pitting Ice Box against her uncle and her own Ivan Drago, Spike Hammersmith. On the final play, in a game of inches, Ice Box stopped him just short of the goal line, and girl power won.

Ice Box was a silver lining in a pop culture education that was altogether awful in representing women. But even if movies like *Little Giants* and *The Mighty Ducks* would throw an errant bone in the form of a token Black boy, kids' media did even less for Black girls. I snuck to watch television meant for viewers above my age range, and what I learned about women was worse.

I watched *The Crush*, where Alicia Silverstone played an obsessed girl with a crush on an older man. When he didn't reciprocate her love, she took a used condom from his trash bin, put it inside herself, and accused him of rape.

I watched an episode of *Roseanne* that began with a spinning camera of disorientation as John Goodman looked at the calendar to realize that Roseanne was on her period. It was a type of survival episode where he had to endure Roseanne's bizarre behavior until her period would end.

I watched *A Thin Line Between Love and Hate*, starring Martin Lawrence and Lynn Whitfield, about a womanizing man who seduced a woman by telling her that he loved her. After realizing his manipulation, she went unhinged and tried to murder him, an attempt he survived.

What I was learning about white women in the real world

though seemed to agree with what I had seen on TV, and the same felt true for white suburbanites in Michigan. They had more money than us. They had bigger houses than us. When they spoke, it sounded like they thought the world was theirs.

Some of them, like Kyle, wanted what was ours, too. Kyle was known for wanting to be Black and acting accordingly. He was the first white person to say "nigga" in front of me. Brandi and Precious told me about him one morning on the commute before school, and I told them how I had met Kyle in the bathroom the first day I visited Metro. They laughed their way through stories about Kyle, one after the other, about the clothes he would wear, the lies he would tell, and how he would always get into trouble, but never *real* trouble, like the kind with consequences, because he was Kyle, and his family went to the church, and he was white. If I was surprised by a story they told of Kyle trying to regale them with his collection of Bone Thugs-n-Harmony, they would laugh with a hand wave that said, "Yeah, that's Kyle, he thinks he's Black." If I was surprised by one where Kyle rapped along with niggas and bitches without getting in trouble, the hand wave would say "What did you expect?" They didn't like it, but they were used to it.

One day during class, DMX began to blare from the back of the classroom where a small row of computers doubled as a computer lab. The school was so small that every space was multipurpose. The gymnasium doubled as the auditorium, eighth and ninth grades shared a classroom, and the classroom doubled as the cafeteria and computer lab. I started to want more friends my age than Brandi who was still a grade below me, and Kyle had wanted me as his Black friend from the day I arrived. It served us both, and I accepted our shared interests with whatever discomfort it brought, so when "Ruff

Ryders Anthem" started playing from the back of the class-room I started to walk over. Mr. Newman, one of my new teachers, was furious.

"Jordan," he said, red in the face. "Turn it off and do it now."

I froze in my tracks. I hadn't even reached the computer yet, let alone been the source of music. I started to protest that it wasn't me, but Mr. Newman cut me off. Then Kyle paused the music and started to laugh.

"He's right, Mr. Newman, it was me," Kyle said.

Aside from the shock of Mr. Newman's accusation, his assumption that I was the obvious source of the disruption, the laughter is what was most memorable. It was the second time I had been accused by a white person for something I hadn't done within my limited experience with white people. The first time was back in a mixed-race Pre-K when a white girl said that I was the one who used crayons in the pencil sharpener, and I cried inconsolably. I cried at the simplicity of the injustice, that someone could say something untrue. She was the one who had ruined the pencil sharpener, and she could simply say it was me to get out of trouble herself.

With Kyle, though, it was his easy smile, his laughter at his own confession that made me want to cry, although I was too old now and knew well enough to hold it back. He wouldn't get in trouble, and he knew it. The prospect of getting in trouble was enough to paralyze me with fear, but Kyle could laugh in the face of it. It was an early lesson, the presumption of guilt, the harsher consequence, and the fear. I had it, and Kyle didn't.

Mr. Newman's apology was the sincere embarrassment of a white Christian who might consider themselves uncor-rupted by racism, but whose racism was laid bare on display to the accused Black boy and the white one aware of his invincibility. And I grew one step closer to the passive hand wave that Brandi and Precious would give when they shared their adventures at Metro, the hand wave that didn't like what happened, but asked "what did you expect?"

After several months at Metro I was more accustomed to my new world. Ms. Samborski said things like "Jesus rocks" and "the love of God is awesome," messages that I knew but with a delivery that was foreign. I started to see my situation as more permanent, gradually abandoning the belief that I would get back to Detroit Urban the same way I gradually abandoned the belief I could get my parents back together. Neither would happen, so I would need to find a new normal.

At home, I would search for it in Cliff.

At school, I became determined to make white friends.

Before moving to a white school, I never considered myself particularly funny. I could be clever, but I wasn't Xavier, Allen, or Terrell back at Detroit Urban, three of my friends who could leave me gasping for air in laughter. The white kids, though, thought I was hilarious.

Insults had been a social skill growing up. I was used to being made fun of and sending retorts back as a normal part of having fun with my friends. Spending time with Darryl's older friends meant losing more than I won, especially as a short, fat kid with an afro who looked like Craig Mack fucked Nintendo's Kirby, as I was once told.

Bringing those types of jokes from Detroit to Plymouth made them new, and even a medium wit was considered a razor-sharp tongue to white Adventists. Instead of searching for Black culture in the media I watched, I started to export it for the friendship it brought.

The cultural currency spent well, so when those "friends"

began to feel comfortable enough to ask how many objects they could hide in my hair, I hid a pencil to show them. Then a chess piece.

Then paperclips.

Then a ruler.

Brandi and Precious were still miles ahead of me. I was embarrassing myself for the entertainment of white people while being embarrassed about their mom being the school janitor. I would take the debris out of my hair when I got home, ashamed enough not to share it with even Darryl, but glad enough to do it again the next day. Whether the white kids were laughing at me or laughing with me, they were laughing.

CHAPTER 11

SEX EDUCATION

The Adventist church's aversion to sexual activity gave me a particularly confusing shame as I went through puberty. Premarital sex was wrong, but I wasn't worried about that as much as "sins of the heart." I was taught that if a man thought something in his mind, then in the eyes of the Lord it was already as if he had done it, and that was heavy pressure for a kid who could see a billboard on his school commute and need to hide his erection. If I thought about sex? Sin. Woke up with an erection? Sin. Lust was an iniquity I couldn't avoid even in my sleep.

But now that I was a teenager, sex was a new social currency, so I pretended to know a lot more than I did.

One day, Mrs. Simon, the school principal who also taught Bible class, passed out an information sheet on what was called a serious topic for the Last Days. The heading read, "Are You Homophobic?"

"He's gay, that's what it means," said a student named Owen, answering the question to another student who was even naiver than me.

Owen was another suburban white kid, but one who was considered a troublemaker for being openly into the things he liked, specifically heavy metal rock music. He was short and skinny, wore baggy black JNCO jeans with a wallet chain, and rode a skateboard. Rumor was that he huffed paint, which was a rumor he seemed okay to nurture regardless of whether it was true or not, but he didn't have "problems," in my estimation. Owing money to someone you couldn't pay was a problem. The cops chasing you was a problem. Being in the wrong neighborhood and getting jumped was a problem. Owen wasn't a problem, he was an Adventist kid who wore black, and I liked him for the same reasons that others made fun of him. I recognized in him the sense of outcast that I saw in myself in this new setting. Then he told me how JNCO stood for "jeans 'n-words' can't own" and I was reminded of my place.

He was wrong about what "homophobic" meant, but he was in line with me and the rest of my friends who had called everything gay.

I didn't know anyone who was openly gay, and I didn't find them at all in the media I watched, so my knowledge of gay people came from weekday usage of the word as a pejorative and weekend warnings against homosexuality from church. One weekend, a Sabbath School teacher at Northwest Seventh-day Adventist Church had told me there were gay spirits trained by Lucifer to deceive young people towards fornication, and even worse homosexuality, and she told me to invoke the name of Jesus to send them running away. But gay people were about as real to me as atheists. They only existed in parables and sermons. Yet here I was being handed a worksheet asking if I was homophobic.

"I need you all to get in groups of three and fill out the

questions on your sheet," Mrs. Simon instructed the class. "Yes, Jessica?"

A hand lowered from the left of the class. "Shouldn't we do this individually? Because it's, like, sensitive or private?"

Mrs. Simon smiled for the class. "Is anyone gay in here?" she asked, scanning the room. "I don't think we need to worry about that, Jessica. But, of course, if anyone feels uncomfortable, please feel free to come talk with me and we'll sort it out."

Jessica and the rest of the class were satisfied with our answer as we began finding partners for our groups. "Yo, I'm definitely homophobic," Kyle whispered to anyone within earshot, and my mind went to a show I had recently started, that I was just beginning to love. I *did* make a gay character. There *was* one, after all. He lived in the city of Townsville.

Cartoon Network's *The Powerpuff Girls* featured a team of Bubbles, Blossom, and Buttercup. The all-girl group of heroes represented an obvious message of empowerment, but one that was still rare in cartoon lineups that marketed a dichotomy of "girl" and "boy" cartoons, games, and toys. Nerf guns and Crossfire commercials for boys, Electronic Dream Phone and EZ Bake Oven commercials for girls. I watched everything I could, though, and fell in love with shows like *The Powerpuff Girls* and *Sailor Moon* that were "girl shows."

I watched as Blossom, Bubbles, and Buttercup volleyed villains back and forth with punches, knocking out their teeth and spraying blood. Buttercup was gross and violent, but was still a girl, while Bubbles talked in a high-pitched voice and loved all things girly, but was also still a girl. Blossom was the smart "fearless leader" type as much as Leonardo or Cyclops. Their diversity of traits was written with a sledgehammer when writing with a sledgehammer was perfect in its function. *The Powerpuff Girls* were a blatant shove against hyper

125

masculinity and passive femininity.

The series swung its hammer at gender expectations with each episode, down to the creation of the Rowdyruff Boys, an evil all-boy analog to the Powerpuff Girls who would lose power when their fragile masculinity was threatened. It challenged perceptions of feminism as well, particularly in an episode called "Equal Fights" where the girls squared up and then quickly backed down against a woman named Femme Fatale, who used a corrupted interpretation of feminism to trick the girls into letting her run rampant throughout the city. The girls learned a mix of both credible and corrupted ideals and needed to speak with the other trusted women in their lives for guidance. In my favorite scene, Buttercup was so distraught over the revelation of patriarchy that she almost caught a body.

"Surely you've noticed female superheroes aren't nearly as revered as male superheroes," Femme Fatale told the girls as they were flying her to jail.

"Sure, they are," Bubbles said brightly, "there's Supergirl, Batgirl—"

"—Merely extensions of their male counterparts," Femme Fatale explained as she hung upside down by her foot as Buttercup carried her.

"Ha!" replied Blossom triumphantly, "There's Wonder Woman, and...um..." Her joy trailed off.

"She's right! There is no one else!" Buttercup yelled so suddenly that she accidentally dropped Femme Fatale from a hundred feet in the air.

And while the scene is an obvious exaggeration of a problem with female representation in media, the episode hit its target by speaking to me about diversity, the ways it could be manipulated, how I had to think critically, and the importance of intellectual support from people I could trust. Not bad for a sledgehammer.

The girls defeated monsters and villains in service to a bumbling nincompoop, a man-child of a mayor whose position was clearly held despite his idiocy and entirely owing to his deputy mayor, another woman, Sara Bellum.

The mayor was the butt of the joke. If not for women, the world would have crumbled to male stupidity, which was just the message in one episode titled "Speed Demon" where the girls flew so fast that they traveled through time to the future. Since they had traveled through a time warp, they had also been absent from the regular time continuum, meaning the city of Townsville was left to fare without them for years. Everything had gone to hell without the Powerpuff Girls, like what would happen to local government if not for Ms. Bellum as the brains behind the blundering mayor.

The single male figure prominent in every episode of the Powerpuff Girls was Professor Utonium, the girls' father figure. The girls were aware they were created in a laboratory by accident.

"He's sort of our dad," the girls would say. "He made us," acknowledging something that could have been cause for embarrassment, but never was. And as their dad, Professor Utonium took the role of homemaker and father in a unique way. He was supportive of the girls making their own decisions in a time where TV fathers were known to be overbearing protectors of their daughters' purity. I had watched countless versions of the angry father answering the door to his daughter's first date or giving a speech explaining how they "know how boys are," but these girls were protectors of the city, often with the professor absentmindedly at home, confident in their safety and success. They weren't daddy's little girls because they needed him, they were daddy's little girls because they loved each other.

One episode dove into the protective-father trope by showing the professor uncharacteristically losing faith in the girls, worrying obsessively over their safety. He stayed up all night building them a giant mechanical warrior in an episode called "Uh Oh, Dynamo," and begged the girls to use it to stay safe. When they eventually conceded to his pleas, Dynamo destroyed the city to the dismay of the mayor and hordes of angry citizens, and a sheepish Professor Utonium learned to fall back. The girls had proven fully capable of making their own decisions, and it was undermining them to reduce their autonomy for his own comfort.

Villains of Townsville were in two categories, keeping the show's format from a basic same-antagonist every week approach or a monster-of-the-week formula by merging the two formats into one. Some episodes covered a brand new one-and-done monster, generally used in episodes focused on a particular theme or to build one of the girls' characters without distraction from a high-profile villain. Still, other episodes brought a recurring cast of familiar faces, the preeminent villains of the city of Townsville like the evil genius and redundant orator Mojo Jojo, the country bumpkin Fuzzy Lumpkins, local teen punks the Gangreen Gang, and the spoiled brat heiress-turned-evil Powerpuff wannabe, Princess.

But there was one villain who was so evil that he was only known by a single name rarely dared to be spoken. In another divergence from traditional villains and gender representation, *The Powerpuff Girls* had an unofficially queer supervillain simply known as "Him."

Him wore black high heel boots up to his knees. Him

wore a tutu and 16th-century ruff around his neck. Him fluctuated his voice between high-pitched feminine tones and deep angry growls, had rosy cheeks, long eyelashes, lobster hands, and a curled goatee. The only way we knew Him to be male was because his name was "Him."

By featuring Him as the most powerful villain, evil enough to be admired by Mojo Jojo and known for being cruel yet comfortable enough to rock six-inch heels and transform into a butterfly, *The Powerpuff Girls* took gender roles on its biggest loop of the rollercoaster. Of course, villainizing queer characters would be overdone in the years to come and would become a trope worth its own dissection. And even for me, his villainy and queerness could have reinforced ideas I had been taught on conflating homosexuality and evil. But Him was great, and he was what I had.

"Me too," I said, after Kyle whispered how he was homophobic. I grabbed my worksheet and the two of us began to move to the back of the room with a few other friends. I was happy to join them, full of the pride that comes with having friends in ninth grade.

"Did you read this shit?" Kyle asked. He read one of the questions, "*what would you do if a gay person sat next to you in church?*" and laughed at the absurdity.

"What would a gay person be doing in church?" I asked.

"Gay people can go to church, they can hide their gayness," a friend added.

"Why would they want to hide their gayness? They would be scared and know they're going to hell, why would they want to be reminded?" My logic was compelling.

"Dude I bet they go to look at guys' asses and jerk off on the balcony," Kyle began. "Because I knew a dude that got caught jerking off on the balcony, and the deacon came up to him and made him leave. And then when he left, they found a stack of gay porn magazines."

The game began. Making up gross stories had become its own social currency among boys, with each one trying to top each other's previous story in an escalating game of one-upmanship, inevitably ending somewhere between scat and incest porn.

"It's gross. Like, how can a guy make you hard?" Kyle said, scrunching his face. "I was stroking yesterday, and they showed the guy's face, and I was like," he groaned and panto-mimed his disgust as the rest of us laughed. "I went completely soft, and I couldn't get hard anymore."

I would listen closest when they would talk about porn, because I hadn't really seen it yet. Before ubiquitous internet access, my access to sex was limited to the magazines I saw in corner stores at home. Somewhere near the general interest magazines was an adult section with Hustler, Playboy, and a dozen lesser-known titles with niches from "barely legal" to "mature" women, from amateur models to porn stars. By law, the racks covered them to hide everything below the name of the magazine, which made stealing a look one of many rites of passage for a city kid, alongside pocketing candy or trying to buy alcohol. But I hadn't seen past their covers.

"I squirted in my eye once," Kyle would say about watch-ing a porn site he found. "I could stroke it to that, nonstop. There's all these categories." I was beginning to recognize the rules of their comedy, the setup, dismount, and the landing. Introducing porn categories was the setup. "There's prego porn, midget porn, every kind of porn. But you know what they don't have?"

I recognized the dismount and searched for a good answer on par with Kyle's imagination.

"Period porn," Kyle said. That was the landing, and I reacted with disgust and joy, there with my new friends, despite knowing little about porn, sex, or periods.

I went back to my worksheet and the question *"What would you do if a gay person sat next to you in church?"*

"I'd move to another seat," I wrote as my answer on the worksheet, proud of my problem-solving.

"I once heard of this kid, he was on a baseball team and they were so gross," Kyle started again. By now I understood that while my social capital came from my Blackness, Kyle's came from his perceived maturity, knowing more stories than the rest of us. "After every game, all the players would put a slice of bread on a bench in the locker room." I immediately knew this story would end with someone eating that bread. "And then they all had to start jerking off over the bread, and whoever was the last person to come, they had to eat it." I made another offering of laughter and disgust in gratitude for meeting my goal of making white friends.

"How many times do you jerk off a week?" Kyle asked. "I probably do, like, twice a day on average. So that's, what, fourteen times a week?"

Friends began to take their turns, sharing how often they masturbated, the porn they watched, how far they ejaculated. Then they looked for me to take my turn.

Maybe it was because I felt confident having new friends, or maybe it was my religious guilt, but for some reason I told the truth.

"Like I said, you all are nasty. I don't do that shit." I had begun the habit of waiting until the end of the day to ask forgiveness of my sins, rather than following each time I cursed. Kyle began laughing hard enough to pull Mrs. Simon's attention.

"Are you boys having a problem over there?" Mrs. Simon raised her nose to peer over the students blocking her line of sight.

"No, sorry, Mrs. Simon," I said. "I'm serious, I don't." I whispered back to my friends.

"Wait, you mean to tell me you've never stroked your cock?" Kyle asked. "He's such a liar."

And I hadn't, until that night.

With a made-for-TV movie and a newfound guilt for not masturbating, I masturbated for what would be the first of many. I began to masturbate everywhere, in my bedroom, my bathroom, your bathroom. No bathroom was safe. A righteous prudishness to sex meant that the church rarely spoke about masturbation in an educational sense, so I didn't have any etiquette for when or where it was appropriate. You either learned from yourself or from kids like Kyle.

American Pie would premiere around the same time, and I would become savvy enough to sneak into a theater on my own after hearing about the teen comedy. It was a cultural touchstone featuring affluent white suburban high school students learning about sex for the first time, meaning it captured the zeitgeist of everything I needed to know. *American Pie* was sex education when my school taught none. It had the raunchy social interactions that I had only begun to learn were the currency of white teens. It answered questions I didn't even know I had, like what lacrosse was. It was an instructional manual for how to be white, affluent, and horny. It was even set in Michigan.

American Pie came on the heels of other late-night cable movies I started to watch on the rare occasion I had access to premium channels with late-night programming. I knew David Duchovny not from *The X-Files*, which I was scared into avoiding for fear of Satanism, but from *Red Shoe Diaries* on Cinemax. Early reality shows like HBO's *Taxicab Confessions* earned my loyalty by rewarding patience with a backseat sex scene before DVRs allowed me to fast forward to what I was searching for. *Sex and the City* frustrated the hell out of me when it proved to have very little of the sex I hoped to find.

B-movies combined sex and TV, and I suppressed my guilt by telling myself that I cared about the movies and that the sex only happened to be part of the experience, no different than hearing bad words in a good movie.

Mid-to-late nineties erotic dramas continued my sex education. *Showgirls* featured the familiar face of Elizabeth Berkley, and Jessie Spano from *Saved by the Bell.* "You can fuck me when you love me," she quipped to Black actor Glenn Plummer, one of the earlier interracial relationships I saw onscreen. Berkley's character, Nomi, was a dancer who dreamed of climbing to stardom, becoming an exotic dancer in Las Vegas along the way. Her swimming pool sex scene was famous, at least in my heart, for the unbridled abandon I imagined sex to offer as she flopped backwards in the water. She was overcome with lust. It was uncontrollable.

Then there was *Species*, about an alien who took the form of a human woman. In her quest to reproduce and propagate her alien species, she took what I was learning to be the most attractive form irresistible to men, young, thin, white, and blonde. I was becoming fluent in the genre of softcore porn that lived under the guise of drama or suspense, a wink-wink agreement between me and film. They knew what they were, and I knew what they were, and we would help each other by colluding in our charade.

Species 2, then Denise Richards and Neve Campbell in *Wild Things*, followed by Sarah Michelle Gellar in *Cruel*

Intentions. They featured young stars familiar from more teen-focused movies and television shows, and they offered deniability to my real motivation for watching them. Then I shed the façade altogether when I won my first adult magazine through Darryl's friend Deshawn, who bought one for me while we were at the corner store.

My sexual miseducation came at a cost though, even worse than wanting women to be Magikarp during sex and believing they would enjoy it. Abstinence-only sex education bathed me in shame for what I watched, and it didn't prepare me for the guilt that would come with betraying the values I had learned in church and at home. For the first few months, I masturbated without a care in the world, fun and fancy-free. But that came to a halt at a youth-focused Bible study on the sins of the flesh and the importance of purity.

Masturbating was a sin, as I had known, but I had conveniently suppressed this until an adult stood before us reminding us of its consequences. As Jesus bore the weight of our sins, we hurt Jesus on the cross with every orgasm, so following each one came the crushing realization of what I had done. The guilt escalated each time I masturbated, until each came with a promise that that time would be the last time. After weeks of obsession, one bout of guilt led me to take the magazine that Deshawn had bought me and set it on fire in the backyard, losing the only pornography I had and replacing it with a promise that I would never masturbate again. The self-promises typically lasted several days, sometimes for weeks, until I would fail, break my oath to God, and cry in my room.

When I found pornography in anime by accident, their intersection would only make things worse. The local video store, Movie Mania, added an anime section that included titles rated NC-17. I didn't know what that meant at first, but I quickly found out.

La Blue Girl was definitely porn, but it avoided the closed-door adults-only section of rental stores. Mom was busy with Cliff, so Darryl and I were given $10 that we spent on Movie Mania every weekend, renting three movies per weekend, one for him, one for me, and one we decided together. At first, we worried we would be turned away for renting movies with ratings higher than PG-13. I was 13 by now and Darryl was 16, but we soon learned that none of the store clerks cared what we rented. We could watch whatever we wanted. The floodgates were open.

Darryl and I would spend hours wandering Movie Mania each Saturday night after the Sabbath ended, walking aisle by aisle, genre by genre. We watched new horror movies each week until we'd seen every *Nightmare on Elm Street*, *Friday the 13th*, and *Hellraiser*. We watched a new action movie each week until we'd memorized *Face/Off*, *ConAir*, and *The Rock*. Spending two or three hours just browsing the titles became completely normal to us, something we didn't realize was overkill until Darryl brought his girlfriend, Viola, who begged us to just pick something and go or she'd hurl herself into traffic.

But *La Blue Girl* and the titles that followed were even more graphic than the magazine I had cherished and then burned, and anime porn became my newest obsession.

It was a springboard into countless other anime, though. I often started by resenting the others, the classic anime like *Akira* or *Ghost in the Shell* that I had chosen expecting them to have nudity. But I began to appreciate those too.

My access to porn became limitless, with plots of tentacle demons and ninjas who could win sexual fealty by making rival ninjas orgasm. But the guilt wasn't far behind.

I realized I had to outsmart the system. God had said "thou shalt not kill," but I knew there were provisions in Exodus 17 for when Moses needed to wage war. When Moses lowered his arms, the Israelites would begin to lose their battle with the Amalekites, but as long as his arms were raised, God favored him in what would otherwise be a sin. Moses needed to kill, and God not only allowed it, but he also helped him. A physical toll was the righteous price for our own imperfection. Eve would labor in childbirth for her sins, Adam would need to toil the land for his, and Jesus would make the ultimate sacrifice for us all through his torture and death. Moses had to suffer exhaustion to stretch God's rules against murder, but with physical sacrifice came grace.

I needed to find my own sacrifice to afford my own grace. I came up with two.

First, I would masturbate without reaching climax, having convinced myself it was okay to masturbate so long as I stopped before finishing. By taking away the ultimate reward of masturbating, I could show my sacrifice to God's will and avoid shame, or even feel pride, from my actions.

And while sometimes it worked, too often it failed. I would fail, and this led me to the second sacrifice of forceful restraint. If the orgasm was the sin, and ejaculation was the orgasm as I knew it, I could stop the ejaculation to keep the sin inside. And that's what I began to do.

I would masturbate until I was near climax and hope to stop, but if I didn't, I would squeeze as hard as I could. I would try rubber bands as well, anything that could keep the semen from escaping, keep the sin where it belonged, and the pain would be the sacrifice. I would try to press the semen down my urethra and back into my body, rolling two fingers inward like sliding toothpaste until it rested in its proper place in the tube.

Loopholes hurt physically. Emotionally, they were a relief.

CHAPTER 12

WHEN YOU BELIEVE

At the same time that I was watching *La Blue Girl*, my mom thought she was catering our media consumption to follow the fruits of the Spirit. "By beholding you become changed" I was taught, so even when she bent the softer rules by bringing us to a movie theater, she had a good reason. She brought Darryl and me to the movie theater on three occasions.

The first time I entered a movie theater was in 1992 to watch *Malcolm X*, Spike Lee's film starring Denzel Washington on the life of the civil rights leader, a three-hour marathon for a seven-year-old in which I fell asleep partway through. The second movie was *The Lion King* in 1996, another Black film, in a way, its Afrocentricity highlighted by mom's reminder that James Earl Jones was Mufasa, and the story was based in the savannah. The third was in 1998 to see *The Prince of Egypt*.

I experienced what I often knew to expect from "Christian entertainment," moral themes from long-memorized Bible stories with Hanna-Barbara animation. What I got instead was a movie that made me feel proud to be both Black and a Christian. *The Prince of Egypt* featured Black characters, an anomaly amongst the usual Biblical representations of people from North Africa and the Middle East.

I was given Moses and Rameses, two brothers who were central to the larger web of relationships I saw throughout the movie. Heir to the throne, Rameses bore the pressure of the greatest dynasty known to the world, while his little brother Moses took it as his job to get the two of them into trouble. Moses was a lighthearted prankster opposite a character with an unnaturally serious demeanor, but they were good friends who brought out the best and worst in one another.

Other relationships included Moses and his father, the man who he learned killed an entire population of children, saying "they were only slaves," and Moses and Miriam, his blood sister who knew who he was since birth, that he was one of those slaves, and who waited for him to live up to his promise.

And then we met Tzipporah. With long black hair and dark skin, even darker than Moses' skin, I saw Moses fall in love with a woman unlike most I'd seen onscreen. A classmate at Metro would call her ugly, saying she had a big face and…I don't know what else he said, I had a stroke. Tzipporah, from willful survivor to supportive friend to loving wife, joined Elisa Maza in my childhood crushes.

When Moses met her for the first time at the royal banquet, she demanded to be set free. "I'm giving you all the respect you deserve," she said. "None."

Moses' mother looked on with sadness and disappointment as Rameses and Moses embarrassed Tzipporah, adding one more layer to what made the characters so special. We met Tzipporah's family and her large bear-like father, Jethro, who was warm and welcoming. We saw Moses and Tzipporah

140

fall in love over the course of Jethro's song, and when Moses told Tzipporah of the burning bush and God's command for him to deliver his people from slavery, Tzipporah said, "I'm coming with you."

It was mesmerizing. It was Goliath and Elisa all over again, but this time they were both real people.

Of course, the film's animated representation was undermined by the all-white cast that hid behind its progress, with the voices of Val Kilmer, Michelle Pfeiffer, Martin Short, Sandra Bullock, and Steve Martin behind dark-skinned faces, but I knew little about anything behind the scenes of an animated film. It also fell into the pitfall of denoting intelligence or royalty by assigning them a British accent, as Ralph Fiennes gave voice to Rameses. Yet despite its shortcomings, I mostly recall what it meant to me in 1998, an Adventist boy who knew the story by heart but was learning it as if it were the first time.

It also had one of the best soundtracks of any animated musical I had ever heard. From "Deliver Us" to "The Plagues," the music held a darker tone than most animated features that balance in a relatively heavy mix of lighthearted songs. In a movie about slaves rebelling in a righteous faith-based campaign for their freedom, strong and emotional was what the musical score called for. Instead of upbeat songs that prioritized fun, the music replaced "fun" with an equally compelling and more powerful feeling of hope. Each song conveyed the painful emotion of their lives as slaves, the faith needed to have to risk lives against the Pharaoh, and, in Moses' case, the conflict of betraying his brother. To this day, few songs capture the spirit of a movie as well as when Whitney Houston and Mariah Carey sang the Academy Award-winning Best Original Song, "When You Believe."

The opening scenes were enough to melt me into puddles, watching Egypt built on the backs of slaves, as the chorus demanded the deliverance they were promised. Later, when the VHS was available, I repeatedly rewound a three-second scene of an old man who crumbles from the toil of the day, reaches up, and grasps the outstretched hand of a young man who helps him up, only for both to be shoved back to work by an overseer. And they weren't even the main characters.

It started with a desperate mother, Yocheved, and her two children, Aaron and Miriam, walking through the reeds to the Nile River. Pretend you don't know the story already. Imagine it, if you can, with a fresh mind. A tyrannical dictator, to protect his throne, ordered the murder of thousands of children. Here is a mother so broken in despair that she is willing to take a basket, line it with tar, and place her newborn inside of it to take its chances with the Nile.

Can you imagine the hopelessness? The thought that your child's one percent chance of survival in a river is better than your child's guaranteed death at the hands of a city guard with a dagger? From a desperate Yocheved laying her son in the basket, to the moment Moses raised his arms, closed his eyes, and drove his staff into the waters of the Red Sea, *The Prince of Egypt* was an emotional adventure that rivals any drama I have watched since. It exemplified the power of faith not only for Christians, but for anyone who allowed themselves to be inspired. It's a story of hope and triumph, loss, grief, and family. Moses, an outcast and vagabond, found redemption after feeling as lost as I could have ever felt in my life.

How tragic was it that his redemption was sparked by his birth sister but required the betrayal of his adoptive brother? How beautiful that he fulfilled his sister's naïve wish that she sang to a baby in a basket. "I have a prayer just for you. Grow, baby brother, come back some day. Come and deliver us, too."

The Prince of Egypt was the biggest surprise of my childhood. And it showed Black people at the forefront of it all.

Back at home, our evening family worships had gone from brief Friday night prayers at sundown to bring in the Sabbath, to longer nights that included songs, scripture readings, and a round robin where each of us shared a testimony from the week. It lasted at least half an hour and ended with us on our knees, our elbows to the sofa cushions, hands clasped together as we took turns praying aloud, youngest to oldest, wife, then Cliff.

Back at school, when I got to ninth grade at Metro I started transitioning away from friends like Kyle and towards ones like Mike Thomas, a half-white half-Asian kid who I'd become close with over a mutual love of sports and comedy. Mike was the funniest person I knew, the type whose silliness cloaked the fact that he was the smartest person in the room. His grades were a quarterly reminder that he took school more seriously than his humor would suggest, straight A grades to bookend three months of boob jokes and SNL references.

He would introduce me to *South Park*, and later, animation that lived deeper in the bowels of internet culture than I had ever waded on my own. There was a flash-animated series called *Salad Fingers* where a mutated man spoke erotically about rusty spoons. There was another called *The Milkman* about a friendly neighborhood man spontaneously assaulting a woman in her home and shooting her young son when he walks in.

What endeared me to Mike was how much he was like me. His family served vegetarian food. They had evening worships to bring in the Sabbath. Yet here we were, watching *South Park* and making references to Jay-Z lyrics and SNL. He knew what it was like to walk between pious Adventism and the non-Adventist world. He was even a more extreme version of me. His father wasn't Mr. Thomas, he was *Pastor* Thomas, making Mike a PK, a pastor's kid. And despite being a PK, or perhaps because of it, Mike would say and do non-Adventist things I had never said or done. He was proof they could be said and done.

Mike and I would talk for hours on the phone, cracking jokes and gossiping about classmates. Cliff would get upset at his phone calls, and about my increasing time spent on the phone in general, but especially when Mike would call during worship.

"Doesn't his family close the Sabbath?" Cliff would ask. To Cliff, Pastor Thomas' whiteness outranked his Adventist-ness and he needed to get his house in order, instead of letting his son run wild, calling people on the Sabbath.

I wasn't embarrassed about Mike, though, because he knew it was the Sabbath. He just didn't care.

It was different from when I was in Elementary school and my best friend at Detroit Urban, Jason, spent the weekend at my grandma's house when we were in fourth grade. On Friday night we had worship, with mom, grandma, Darryl, Jason, and me going through the singing, scripture reading, and prayers despite Jason not being Adventist or observant of the Sabbath. When it came time to pray, Jason joined us with his knees bent, elbows on the sofa cushions, hands clasped, and eyes closed.

This was before Cliff, so we hadn't started praying youngest to oldest, working our way towards the head of household. Instead, we'd go popcorn style, or one person would pray aloud for all of us. But when it was my mom's turn to pray, I heard someone mumbling. I kept my eyes closed, not wanting to break reverence, but when it continued, I slowly opened my eyes and stole a peek to the side. Jason was praying aloud during someone else's prayer, trying to keep up with this ceremony he'd never seen before.

I wanted to stop him, to tell him he was doing it wrong, that we were supposed to be listening, but what could I do? We were in the middle of prayer. I wondered what my grandma was thinking as she heard it, and what my mom was thinking as she tried to pray and was being interrupted by my friend. Would I get in trouble? Would we have to go witness to his family?

He had been trying to keep up the whole night, I realized. He didn't know the songs, or the Sabbath. He probably went to church on *Sunday*. I was as embarrassed for Jason as I would be for myself the next day, though. At my grandma's house, Jason was the weird one, but at school, if he told our friends, the weird one would be me. I considered it the greatest act of fourth grade best-friendship grace that Jason never spoke of it.

Years later it would be Mike who interrupted my family's evening worships, but he would be different because he understood. I could tell him that we were having worship, and that Cliff would get upset, and Mike would laugh, and he would understand. We would grow closer from it. He got it. He knew both sides. He was even non-white. There was something good about this Adventist school thing, I thought. There was Mike.

I missed Jason, Xavier, Terrell, and the rest of my friends at Detroit Urban. I missed our mean jokes at each other, our camaraderie against our teachers, our recesses of tackle football outside in the summer and basketball indoors in the winter. At Metropolitan Junior Seventh-day Adventist Academy, I was still a novelty to most kids who weren't like Mike, Brandi, or Precious. And to the teachers, I was automatically worse.

One day I sat with my new friends, fidgeting with the plastic silverware in our classroom that doubled as our cafeteria for lunch. I had broken three prongs of a plastic fork, and as I realized what it resembled, I laughed as I lifted the fork, putting on display a plastic fork with only its second prong remaining. It was a middle finger, the plastic fork version, to anyone with an imagination. Mr. Newman saw, and told Mrs. Simon, and Mrs. Simon began writing a letter.

Bringing the letter home that night, guilt flooded over me as I told my mom I had been suspended from school. My mom and Cliff were invited to the principal's office for a conversation about my behavior.

It was my first time I had ever been suspended from school. I had gotten paddles at Detroit Urban, but I had also won awards for good behavior and perfect attendance, and had never gotten below a C, let alone been suspended. I realized that at Metro, though, I was just the poor Black student from Detroit. It had become my new, third identity that trumped the others. I was the Black kid. Black, as in urban. Black, as in the kid who knows rap. Black, as in token Black. Black, as in fast. Black, as in slow. Black, as in first to be chosen in pickup on the first day. Black, as in impressive when achieving above expectations. Black, as in intimidating. Black, as in angry. Black, as in a curiosity. Black, as in deserving to be suspended from school for a middle finger from a plastic fork. I wasn't a nerd, or an Adventist, I was Black.

I spent my suspension at home, technically on punishment, but since mom and Cliff were at work and Darryl was at school, I watched *La Blue Girl*.

That day, I would later find out, would bring even more guilt than being suspended for a middle finger from a broken plastic fork.

CHAPTER 13

1-800-WET-GIRL

I never felt good enough to be saved. Being good enough, worthy of salvation, was simultaneously an expectation and a never-ending, impossible quest.

I spent my time watching cartoons, waking up as early as six in the morning to watch *Mighty Max*, *Pokémon*, or *James Bond, Jr*. I tagged along with Darryl and Deshawn, but sometimes they would ditch me to spend time with teens their own age. When I was left home alone, I started to dial 1-800 numbers that I had learned from the magazine Deshawn had bought me and listen to the recorded messages of phone sex lines before they'd ask for a credit card.

Since I lit the magazine on fire in the backyard in a bout of guilt, I didn't have the numbers anymore, so I started to guess. I learned their patterns, how to match the letters of the 800-number with the numbers on the dial pad, like 1-800-WET-GIRL. I learned that the phone numbers needed to be at least seven digits, that 1-800-HOT-SEX wouldn't work, but that the words could be slightly longer than seven digits and would still be okay, like 1-800-HORNY-TEEN.

Then I realized I could make up my own word combinations and be right more than half the time, like 1-800-BIG-BOOBS, and that some had longer introduction recordings than others but that they would all eventually end with asking for a credit card that I didn't have.

And then I would masturbate, and then I would feel awful.

I was born into sin and felt my lifelong goal was to be worthy of God's salvation. I owed him. God loved me unconditionally and I needed to love him back, to pay him back for his sacrifice through service, and to follow God's word, lest his sacrifice for me be wasted. The message was always personal. Jesus died for *you specifically*. But I never knew if I was good enough for heaven, and that unknowing only made me eager to please.

After being transferred to Metro I kept in touch with my old friends Jason, Xavier, Allen, and Terrell for a while, those friends I had grown up with at Detroit Urban until my mom's intervention on behalf of the Holy Spirit. I talked with them on the phone and noticed how much more grown-up they were compared to my new friends at Metro. Or rather, how aspirational their maturity was. They were in high school now, while I and the rest of the kids at Metro were in an "Adventist Junior Academy," so their jokes about sex, drinking, or drugs came with more credibility than someone like Kyle.

Except for Jason, my Detroit Urban friends still didn't know about my Seventh-day Adventist background, the Sabbath church services, the evening devotions. They welcomed me regardless of my naiveté though, either because they didn't notice, or were equally naïve and self-conscious, or because we had known each other for so long. I was grateful I still fit in, even if I felt it slipping away as I was exposed less to them and more to the kids in the Metro school at 15585 N Haggerty Road, in Plymouth, Michigan.

Jason, Allen, and Xavier would have different conversations than Justin, Chet, and Kyle. Jason had the names of dead family members on his arm, Justin had frosted tips. While Allen was considering branches of the military, Chet was considering Adventist colleges. Xavier aspired to be a wealthy businessman, but Kyle romanticized the life Xavier already had. My Detroit friends aspired to a better future, one where they were older, more powerful, more in control of their lives. Students at Metro had fewer cares.

My worlds would collide when I was invited to spend the afternoon at Amy Crawford's house. It would be one of my first times visiting a white friend in the suburbs, me hanging out with Amy and her best friend, Jessica Foster.

Jessica was my first crush at Metropolitan Seventh-day Adventist Junior Academy. She was kind and bubbly, with the type of physical traits I was learning that qualified a girl as attractive. Boys were supposed to like thin women with long hair, preferably blonde, and Jessica fit the description. To spend time with Jessica I would also become friends with Amy, talking to them both on the phone for hours. I learned that Jessica's favorite Backstreet Boy was Nick, that she and Amy were allowed to go to a concert once and saw them live. Our incessant conversations were what led to the day where Amy's mom invited me to spend the afternoon with Amy and Jessica at Amy's house.

Amy had a crush on me the same way I had a crush on Jessica. While I was using Amy to get to Jessica, Amy was using Jessica to get to me. After my mom and Cliff dropped me off in the suburbs, Amy, Jessica, and I spent the afternoon the same as we would on the phone, talking about music I had never heard of, and television shows like *Buffy the Vampire Slayer* and *Dawson's Creek* that I had.

Amy's mom was a server at a quick-service restaurant in Michigan called Pita Pit. Ms. Crawford had a brunette mullet, and I saw that in their own way Amy and her mom were different than the other families at school. They weren't affluent. I had not seen a father in Amy's life, nor did I ask. Their house was pretty similar to mine, and they were endeared to me for being different from the other families at Metro.

One of my best friends from Detroit Urban, Allen, called that afternoon when I was first invited to Amy's house, after a phone introduction I had made weeks prior. Allen had been one of the class clowns at school, someone I had known since we were 10 who would get paddles alongside me from our fifth-grade teacher, Mr. Hughes. He also had an older brother, Charles, who was friends with my older brother, Darryl, making us both chubby younger brothers to popular, older brothers on a varsity basketball team.

I had introduced Amy to Allen over the phone several weeks prior, and Amy wanted to know Allen for many of the reasons I suspected she liked me. We were 14 now and interested in relationships, and the appeal of our novelty made us easy to like. This was 1999, DMX's *And Then There Was X* had just come out, and Amy's affinity for the song "Why Do Good Girls Like Bad Guys" made our roles clear. She was the good white girl, we were the roughneck Black boys from the other side of the tracks, and opposites were meant to attract.

In my teens, the divide of popular music was best exemplified by the racism of radio networks. Stations like 96.3 JAMZ, 97.9 WJLB, and 105.9 rotated new hip-hop and R&B, while white stations boasted that they played music without rap. Songs from TLC would play without the Left-Eye verse, and it was advertised openly that the station played "the best new music," but "with no rap," spoken in the deep, echoed voice of a radio DJ.

When I transferred from Detroit Urban to Metro, my music knowledge went from a source of pride to one of chastisement.

"You don't know Kid Rock?" Amy had asked back in school.

I listened to rap, I told her.

Mark, the class's country bumpkin who earned the nickname "Hillbilly Mark," commented that "rap" is one letter short of the words "crap" and "rape."

Like other areas of my life, music would be split into two. On one side was DMX's debut album, *It's Dark and Hell Is Hot*. Lil Wayne debuted *The Block Is Hot*, Mos Def and Talib Kweli presented *Blackstar*, Big Pun released *Capital Punishment*, TLC did *FanMail*, Missy had *Da Real World*, Eve dropped *Ruff Ryders' First Lady*, Destiny's Child debuted *Writings on the Wall*, Jay-Z had *Hard Knock Life: Vol 2*, Outkast released *Aquemini*, Lauryn Hill had *Miseducation*, and there was Biggie's posthumous album, *Born Again*.

I knew them each by heart, their notes, their lyrics, and their adlibs.

On the other side would be Backstreet Boys' *Millennium*. Brittney Spears debuted *...Baby, One More Time*. Christina Aguilera released her self-titled album. Blink-182 had *Enema of the State*, Korn released *Follow the Leader*. Limp Bizkit dropped *Significant Other*. Creed had *Human Clay*, and there was Linkin Park's *Hybrid Theory*."

There were bridges between the two, exceptions that made it clear that a radio station's "no rap" was less a rule than code speak for saying that the station was safe from certain kinds of Black musicians. Eminem, Fred Durst, and Mike Shinoda would close the gap between how I saw my old and new worlds. Local musicians like Kid Rock, Uncle Kracker, and Eminem were especially important, the essence of white, suburban Michigan captured in Uncle Kracker's "Drift Away" music video, his auto-shop jumpsuit, his blue-collar-meets-country-music aesthetic, his soul patch and frosted tips, his hugging a Black musician at the end. Kid Rock's *Devil Without a Cause* was the first time I heard a white person rap "nigga" without hesitation or consequence. I knew them vaguely, limited to the extent I had access to cable to watch TRL.

I would memorize Eminem's *The Slim Shady LP*, and Rage Against the Machine's *The Battle of Los Angeles*. When I ran out of money for music, which was quickly, I turned to Columbia House as my first debt owner. Advertisements for Columbia House music clubs spread throughout magazines offering 12 CDs for the price of one. The small print was having to buy an additional number of albums at the full price of about $20, but with an entire year to meet the commitment. The offer was easy bait for teens who combined a need for fast gratification with low impulse control. I signed up in my name, and my brother's as well for good measure, giving me 24 CDs ripe for the choosing.

The name Smash Mouth was familiar, so their album *Astro Lounge* was added to my list. There was a band called Garbage, and another called Godsmack. I ticked the boxes by their name and would sort it out later. Uncle Kracker's "Follow Me," Train's "Drops of Jupiter," and a flood of other songs would fill the chasm until the distance between the two cultures was as easy as my morning commute. Mike's favorite band was Blink-182, so I would listen to a lot of them. I could travel from the city to the suburbs, between 105.9 to 95.5, as easily as a turned knob on the radio dial.

My mom would be impressed by the Holy Spirit yet again, this time to take a closer look at my music after she noticed my growing CD collection. She sat on my bed and turned the pages of my music folder, inspecting each artist name and album title one by one. She didn't know a single artist or reputation, so she would cull my collection based on names and album art. I could explain an innocuous-sounding name and she believed me and allowed me to keep them. Other names, like Bone Thugs-n-Harmony and Mac 10, were goners. She took at least fifty CDs and I would rebuild my collection in the coming months with more subscriptions to music clubs.

One of the most meaningful albums at the time was Mos Def's *Black on Both Sides*. I was just barely old enough to understand its message and mastery, but I felt encouraged by Mos Def's radical love of Blackness against a culture that taught us not to love ourselves. The album cover was simply his dark-skinned face, plain for all to see. The back of the album was the back of his head, his hair in cornrows. His song "Mr. Nigga" would express what I was feeling, what I didn't have the vocabulary to explain to myself. Regardless of how well I would do in school, it wouldn't matter. Regardless of how many Bible verses I memorized, or that I knew the names of all 66 books of the Bible by heart, in order, it wouldn't matter. Regardless of how well I spoke, or that I never smoked, drank, did drugs, or had sex, it wouldn't matter. I would still be a Black boy around people who have their mind made up about Black boys.

In the closing bars of the "Mr. Nigga" song, Mos Def raps, "I'm a live though, yo I'm a live though. I'm putting up the big swing for my kids, yo. Got my mom the fat water-front crib, yo. I'm a get her them pretty bay windows. I'm a cop a nice home to provide in. A safe environment for seeds to reside in. A fresh whip for my whole family to ride in. And if I'm still Mr. Nigga, I won't find it surprising."

Not surprising at all.

Amy, Jessica, and I spoke from Amy's bedroom, the three of us huddled around her bedroom landline. Allen asked what we were doing and what we were talking about. He didn't have a frame of reference for our topics, for the Backstreet Boys *Millennium* album, for the white teen television dramas I had learned. Amy and Jessica's cultural education was different from Allen's, and Allen's was different from theirs, and I stood in the middle as a cultural translator, filling in the gaps. Some topics would be lost in translation, like when Amy talked about hockey, since I didn't know anything about hockey except that the Red Wings were good enough for Detroit to be called Hockeytown and their games were the only time I would see white people in the city. But I translated well. I felt proud of my friendship with Allen, knowing that the novelty we held to these white girls made us interesting, made us the cool kids, without being old enough or smart enough to understand what comes with that admiration, the reduction of yourself to satisfy what white people wanted, that it could never be worth the cost.

It was perhaps only a matter of time until Allen would lean on the crutch of teen boy humor, leaving me stuck in translation.

"You over there getting blowjobs from white girls?" he asked. It was over the landline in Amy's bedroom where me, Amy, and Jessica sat huddled around the phone.

Time froze, one of two times it would freeze that afternoon.

What could I say? Allen didn't actually expect we were

involved sexually no more than he himself was sexually active. We were both young, immature, inexperienced, misfit ugly ducklings of the younger brother variety. We were in ninth grade. I had barely even kissed a girl, just a peck on the lips with Shanae Martin at Detroit Urban during a game of spin-the-bottle.

The "right" response was out of the question. After years of laughing at similar jokes, telling Allen that his joke wasn't funny just because it was told in the wrong company would have felt like be a betrayal. It would have meant siding with Amy and Jessica and throwing Allen under the bus. I had rarely pushed back on Allen, and I especially didn't want to here, not when I knew that he was joking, that he was only trying to impress, that it was a stupid joke to the wrong audience from a well-intentioned kid. To him, it would seem as if I changed, like I was choosing sides, and that I had left my old friends behind to side with the corny whites and their corny humor. And he wouldn't have been completely wrong.

He spoke it clear as day, *"You over there getting blowjobs from white girls?"* It was unmistakable. I couldn't pretend like I didn't hear it. Besides, what would stop him from repeating the question, asking again? Nothing would stop him. He wouldn't be satisfied if his hilarious question went unanswered. Should I use Amy and Jessica as cover? I was worried about their discomfort. Should I tell Allen that these girls were too innocent for that joke, that it would offend them, go over their heads? Not me though, I'm with you Allen, it's only they're not on that level yet, is that what I should say? Amy and Jessica would find Allen's joke gross after all. Or would they? Was this the novelty they yearned for, boys from the city talking about sex, even if we were clueless, faking it? Would the three of them team up to make fun of me as the inexperienced one, the stupid one, as the people I had brought together created a separate team and leave me out of it, too childish to handle a simple blowjob joke? Like most crass jokes likely to fly over my head, I just wanted the moment to pass, to be over, to go back to safer waters.

By now a few seconds had past but my mind was suspended in anime time, what was a few seconds in real time was half an hour in my head. And at the end of the episode, I laughed. My response would be the one I'd fallen back on for years, an awkward chuckle. Cowardly but faithful. I looked at Amy and Jessica, both seemingly oblivious of the nightmare that had passed. Their mood was still pleasant, neither of them was angry or in tears. The moment passed, my head was above water. I climbed from the water, and onto the ice.

Time stopped for the second time when we heard another voice on the landline. The voice was loud in the way landline phones amplified the volume of those in the same house. It's why when I would try to eavesdrop on my older brother's conversations, I would lift the phone slowly, hoping to avoid the telltale click of the phone, and immediately hold mute.

"Hang up the phone," Amy's mom said. "Right now."

Worse than Amy and Jessica judging my friend, Ms. Crawford had heard Allen joking about blowjobs, about her teenage *daughter* giving blowjobs. Whatever response Amy and Jessica might have had to him being crass, a parent's response would be worse. How could I be so stupid as to worry about Amy and Jessica? I thought about Allen getting in trouble, about him never being able to speak with my new friends again. I thought about how stupid I was for trying to bring these two worlds together, and why I kept them separate. I thought about getting in trouble for having a friend like that, for listening to his jokes, and worse, for laughing along.

Amy, Jessica, and I were sent to the living room where we listened as Ms. Crawford called my mother and Cliff to pick me up early. The minutes felt like hours, the terror of my mom hearing what Allen had said, her embarrassment of the company I kept, her embarrassment of me. The consequences terrified me as well. Would I be on punishment for weeks? For months? Would I be banned from using the phone? Would I be banned from being friends with Allen, from speaking with any of my old friends? Would I lose that part of myself entirely, have it taken away from me? Would I be made to change schools again? I spent the longest years of my life inside that one hour in the suburbs, my heart in throat, my stomach churning.

My mom and Cliff pulled in front of the house, on the street. They stayed inside the car, and as I quietly climbed into the back of the maroon Chrysler minivan, I had a glimmer of hope they would drive off, that we would avoid the confrontation of what happened, the embarrassment of it. But Ms. Crawford was on her way. Cliff was in the driver's seat and rolled down the passenger-side window where my mom sat.

"Jordan got a phone call from his friend, Allen," she said. "And he and Allen," she began to choke up. Her face was angry, and she began to cry. I waited for the axe to fall. "He and Allen were bragging about my daughter giving Jordan a blowjob." I looked up, shocked.

"I didn't say that!" I blurted out, stunned at this version of what happened.

"You did," she said, thrusting her finger at me. She smeared the tears from her eyes. She redirected her attention to my mom and stepfather. "And I just thought you should know."

I don't recall what my mom said, or Cliff, after Ms. Crawford turned to walk away. I know I defended myself, tried to clarify what Allen had asked and how I had laughed, but the whole time I was explaining I was simultaneously trying to wrap my own mind around what had just happened. Ms. Crawford said that it was *my* joke. She said it was *me*, that *I* was *bragging* about getting a blowjob.

For Cliff, this was yet another entry into a growing mound of evidence that I was only a problem for my mother, and further reason why she needed him, our family's new patriarch, to save her from such problems. She had done a poor job raising me, but it was okay, because he was in our lives now and our world was better under his rule.

My mom, for her part, asked me the type of unanswerable questions she was wont to do, asking me to explain myself in a way that I didn't have the language to achieve in the backseat of the car wondering how an adult could have accused me of something I didn't do. I had been so worried about white people looking down on Allen, and on me by association, that it never occurred to me we wouldn't be seen as any different. I wouldn't be afforded the nuance of *Allen* saying one thing and *me* saying another. To Ms. Crawford, whatever Allen had said, I had said too.

Cliff's subsequent lectures felt muted in the background compared to the volume of my mom's silence. Losing phone and TV privileges felt like a formality, my real punishment was the silent heartbreak from my mom and a letter I found on the kitchen table for me later that week. My mom had handwritten it, explaining how she had tried to raise me to be a good son, and had failed. She said she would pray for me, but that being a good son, a good Christian, a good person, would be left up to me. I sat in my bed as I read her letter, the confirmation of my fears of how she might see me. It was a validation of my fear that Cliff had won.

I decided to write her back, spending two days crafting my response. Writing it had become an outlet for some of the anger I felt from feeling so misunderstood, so I tried to defend myself and share who I felt I was, a kid who was trying his best. I left it for her in the same place she had left her note for me. When she read it later that evening, the conversation that followed was brief. She called me into the living room, sat me on the couch, and told me that I was wrong. And then I agreed, and said I was sorry. She tore up my letter and dismissed me, and I went back to my bed and cried. Cliff didn't even need to be there.

In the weeks to follow I lived in constant fear at school. I worried Amy's mom would tell Jessica's mom and other parents. I worried the parents would tell the teachers, that the parents and teachers would warn their kids. In another hard-learned lesson, I learned that Amy and Jessica would remain largely quiet. They wanted to be my friend and they agreed I didn't say what Ms. Crawford said I did, but they wouldn't speak on my behalf, either.

Thinking back on that day with Ms. Crawford, sometimes I still want to convince her of what I said, and why. Even with my understanding as an adult, I struggle with the reality of that day. A white woman lied, I was not believed, and it contributed to the fracturing of my mother's faith that I was more than just one of the bad things in her life, another trouble from which Cliff would claim he could save her from by teaching Darryl and me the discipline we needed. I still want to prove to Ms. Crawford that what she said was wrong, for her to go back and tell my mom that she got it wrong, that I'm not that boy, for my mother to believe I'm not that boy, so that maybe in the future she would believe me when I told the truth.

I still want the validation that my experience was real, that my memory is real. But Darryl wasn't there. He was back on earth while I was lost in Avalon.

Eventually a combination of desperation and bravery led me to the last resort as an intimidated Black boy pleading his case to an adult white woman, I wrote Ms. Crawford a letter, just as I had written my mom. I explained my reaction. I explained what I said. I explained what I didn't say. I explained that I understood what she thought she heard, but that what she thought she heard was wrong.

I was shaking when I gave it to her after school one day, the first time I had dared to approach her since the day she told my mom her version of the story. I had feared her the way any child fears an adult, the way a Black boy would fear an adult white woman who knows her power over him. But my need to convince her, to feel that approval, outweighed even that fear over what she could do to my life. I gave her the letter. She never responded.

CHAPTER 14

TATTOOS AND BRAIDS

Metropolitan SDA Junior Academy only offered school-ing through the ninth grade, which is what "Junior Academy" meant in the Adventist world, that the school was meant to funnel students through a pipeline to a larger academy in the region. In Michigan, that pipeline led to Great Lakes Adventist Academy, or "GLAA," spoken as a word, "Glah." GLAA was the premiere Adventist boarding school for white Adventists in Michigan, and where Metro was a commute to the suburbs, GLAA was a four-hour drive away in *actual* rural Michigan, in the middle of nowhere in the center of the state, at a place called Cedar Lake. At $15,000 a year and having the highest standards for Christ, I actually wanted to go there for my last three years of school. I hadn't spoken with my old friends since the trauma from Allen, and GLAA would be where most Metro students would be going. There were about a dozen of us who were expected to make the transition from the Junior Academy to GLAA.

To afford GLAA, though, wouldn't be easy, and Cliff hated the idea from the beginning. For starters, it would be expensive, but also my leaving would mean that he would have one fewer person to demonize to keep his hold on my mom and maintain his role in the family. Darryl would be leaving for college that same year to attend Andrews University, and if I left too, the nest would be empty. What good was he to our mom if not a father for her sons? What good was it being the patriarch of our house if there was no one over which to rule?

Cliff grew more aggressive that year as he saw us begin to slip away. He would criticize us for being home too often, or not home enough. He would criticize us for being too lazy. He would criticize the food we ate. That year, Darryl would buy the issue of SLAM magazine with his favorite basketball player, Allen Iverson, on the cover, and his second favorite player, Latrell Sprewell, would lead the Knicks to the NBA Finals. Cliff made it a point to hate them both.

One day, he would walk into Darryl's bedroom as Sprewell missed a free throw.

"Maybe he wouldn't miss so much if he didn't have all those tattoos," he said. He hated players with tattoos and braids, the ones he said made our race look bad. Both Darryl and I had braids. The rest was implied.

What I hadn't noticed, though, was that Darryl had stopped laughing at Cliff's abuse. He had been seething at it instead, each new criticism adding to a powder keg. I had never seen Darryl lose his temper, but that summer, I did.

Cliff came home one day and called us into the kitchen to bicker, and for the first time, Darryl started to bicker back. Then Darryl raised his voice. Then Darryl fucking yelled. I watched Darryl storm through the house, ranting and raving about everything that Cliff had ever done and everything he ever said. Darryl yelled, and yelled, and yelled as Cliff stood in the kitchen, at first defending himself and then turning silent when it was clear that Darryl wasn't going to stop.

Darryl banged on the table as he mocked Cliff's criticisms to his face. He banged on the walls as he recounted Cliff's hypocrisies. If it came to blows, I had little doubt that my older brother was going to rip his fucking head off.

He was Gohan yelling "I've had enough of you, Frieza!"

He was Goliath with his eyes red.

He was Optimus saying "Never."

We had never stood up to Cliff before, but here was Darryl, unafraid and fed up, standing up to the biggest bully we'd ever known.

I had never seen anything like it before. I didn't know that we had that in us, and I felt strong in seeing my brother be strong.

Cliff got in his car and drove off, not to return for hours. Mom hadn't been home, so I was sure that Cliff would tell her what had happened to leverage some kind of retaliation against Darryl, against the both of us, but he didn't. When nothing happened, I realized how Cliff had always been wrong and that *he knew it all along*, and to tell my mom about it would be to open the door for sharing everything Darryl had said about him. He kept silent because he was ashamed. This was what his shame looked like. Darryl was right, and he knew it.

Later, Cliff would have the chance to leverage himself over us again, and it would be my fault.

One day, Cliff and my mom walked downstairs carrying a phone bill for over $1,000. My mom asked if we knew anything about it, but she assumed it was an error, something that Cliff would have to sort out over the phone with the phone company. Darryl denied knowing anything about it, and I did, too. Only I was breathing heavy.

After calling the phone company who that assured Cliff that it wasn't a mistake, they explained the source of the charge. They were from phone sex lines.

Mom and Cliff came back downstairs and called Darryl and me out of our room. They asked if we knew anything about phone sex lines, and as we shook our heads "No," Cliff had already come to his conclusion that it must have been Deshawn using their phone line. He had never trusted Deshawn, who met Cliff's criteria for someone who made our race look bad, and he had been looking for a reason to keep him out the house and to ban us from hanging out with him.

But I knew that the bill was real, and that it was from me.

Back when I was calling toll-free phone sex lines, I had escalated from listening to the introduction recordings to attempting to dial random credit card numbers when the recording would end. That never worked, though, and I would try dialing 1-*900* numbers instead of 1-*800* numbers, but they didn't work, either. But there had been one other type of phone number in the back of the porn magazine I had, and those were 011 numbers. And one of them actually worked.

When I was finally connected, I was too scared to talk, so I eavesdropped on a conversation that was mostly indecipherable mumbling. When a phone sex worker finally spoke, I got scared and hung up. What I didn't know was that it had worked because 011 numbers were international calls, and the clock had begun ticking from the moment I dialed, racking up what I learned was a $1,000 phone bill several months later.

After the incident with Amy's mom, I decided I couldn't take another hit. *We* couldn't take it, Darryl and me, after my big brother stood up to Cliff on our behalf. The idea of getting caught with this would be validation of everything Cliff had believed about me, about us, that we were out of control, and my mom would be heartbroken knowing that despite her best efforts, one of her sons still turned out to be a horrible person. I was such a horrible person.

I told myself that Deshawn could fend for himself. He had truth on his side, so if they wanted to believe it was him, they would never be able to prove it. I told myself that he could afford to take the hit because their opinion of him couldn't have been lower anyway. When they suggested to Darryl and me that it might have been Deshawn who made the calls, I nodded.

I had lied to mom and Cliff, and even to Darryl by omission, though he might have known it as we laid together in our shared twin-sized bed and I couldn't control my breathing. I was terrified and heaved on the back of his neck, aware that he could feel the rise and fall of my chest, but unable stop it, to breathe normally. Thinking back, it was a kindness from my brother. He had to know, but he didn't say anything. He didn't leave me, even after we heard mom and Cliff come back downstairs later that night with their discovery.

Cliff had checked the dates and times of the phone calls, and cross referenced them with the dates I was suspended from school for breaking the prongs of the plastic fork. The calls were made that afternoon on the day I was suspended, when no one was home but me.

Mom and Cliff sent Darryl back to our room and took me alone into the living room. We sat on the couch, me looking down at the ground, tears already falling, embarrassed at what I had done, embarrassed that I lied about it, embarrassed I would let them blame Deshawn, embarrassed I got caught.

Cliff started the conversation. He told me about his struggles when he left the church. He said how he would spend hours on phone sex lines and in nightclubs. How he understood. How he had been there, and how it would be okay.

And that was it.

Maybe it was because of Darryl's tirade, or perhaps I really did remind him of what he felt was a low point in his life, but Cliff was empathetic. He was soft. When we sat on the living room couch at what felt like the lowest moment of my life, I expected his fury, but Cliff was kind. And I loved him for it.

PART THREE

"Train up a child in the way he should go, and when he is old he will not depart from it." - Proverbs 22:6

"The Piccolo that you know is gone." - Piccolo

CHAPTER 15

HEALTHY CHOICES

If I was going to go to GLAA, Cliff and my mom agreed that I would have to earn some money for it. During previous summers I had gone door to door with my lawnmower, dried cars at a nearby car wash, and worked at a Taco Bell for money, but given Cliff's work as a Bible salesman, I was to begin door-to-door sales of Bibles and Christian books that summer to help pay for school. Cliff was staunchly Adventist, but he resented how much private schools cost and he hated even worse that I would learn from white people. He shared his negative opinions about white people as much as he did about Black people, and it was just one of the endless ongoing jokes that Darryl and I had about how Cliff was a bigot who hated everyone, including himself.

One day he came home and was excited about a program that he claimed to have pulled special strings to get me in. I was to pack my bags right away and move to a summer program where I would sell Christian books door to door across Michigan. I would be thrown into the deep end of the Colporteur Ministry, where Adventists distributed literature to spread the good word. I cried, just the way I had when my mom woke me up that morning to tell me I would be going to the Metro school for eighth grade, but by then I knew that any protests would be futile and that my mom would go along with whatever Cliff insisted on.

It would be easier to just pack my bags.

When I arrived in a nice townhouse complex just outside of Troy, Michigan, I met a small group of six other Adventist kids and our two group leaders. For five days a week that summer, we would load into a minivan and drive to a preplanned neighborhood to sell Adventist books. Each of us had a walkie-talkie, presumably for safety, but more to say "amen" or "praise the Lord" when we made a sale. In the evenings, after walking in the sun for six to eight hours a day, we memorized our scripts word for word.

At each door, I was taught to lead with a cookbook called *Healthy Choices*. I knew the tactic, and sure enough, the health message was our gateway to more directly Adventist books like *Angels Among Us*, *The Great Controversy*, and the Bible. I carried seven different books in my tote bag and would call on the walkie-talkie to restock after I had sold out. Although I didn't like being a "Colporteur," I was good at it, being young and brave enough to charm sympathetic people into inviting me into their homes and buying a book for $15 to $30.

The program lasted ten weeks and walking for miles a day for eight hours resulted in noticeable weight loss. That weight loss coincided with my teen growth spurt, and by the end of the summer I was suddenly tall and skinny, along with a newfound bravery in talking with strangers.

I could sell water to a well, and it helped endear me to Cliff. As much as I could have hated him, I still wanted his approval, so for the last few weeks before I left for boarding school at GLAA, I joined Cliff to sell Bibles and books on new routes in the Detroit area. It was just he and I on opposite sides of the street, going door to door in the way I had trained all summer. And on those days, I made more money for him than he made for himself. He bragged to my mom about how good I was, but he also began to chastise me again for things unrelated to the Colporteur Ministry, as if going back to his true nature, or to keep my ego in check, or both.

That fall, Darryl left for college, and I left for GLAA.

I looked for refuge in Kyle after Cliff and mom dropped me off on campus. Back at Metro we had played basketball together, rapped music lyrics, and he was one of the closer friends I could access at GLAA since Mike was a year younger and hadn't yet graduated from Metro to GLAA. Before arriving to boarding school though, Kyle had shed his interest in being Black. I approached him on Welcoming Day when all the students arrived on campus to move into dorm rooms. Once the move-ins were done, students spent most of our time on the quad in the beautiful fall weather. There were large clusters of groups full of white students talking in ways that would have been foreign to me only two years ago.

This was the first day of building cliques, choosing best friends, and finding your place in the social hierarchy, so when I found Kyle, I was surprised to see how he was dressed. He was wearing something like board shorts, without a backwards hat. He wasn't wearing a hat at all. He was laughing with a group of other white students of the upper-middle class suburban variety, and it came as a sort of proclamation when he recognized my confusion.

"Oh, yeah, I'm white now," he said.

I wished Brandi and Precious were there to see this. I would have asked if this happened a lot or if it was the first time, but they had finished Metro and gone to public school afterwards instead of GLAA, so when Kyle went from pretending to be Black to wearing polo shirts and board shorts, I had to understand it on my own. He had returned to the safety of being white, like he had finished his long form parody and was ready to move on. It was my first experience with the adopting and subsequent shedding of Black culture by whites who saw our culture as a matter of convenience.

Kyle put one arm around me, leaning his weight into it as he slacked his posture, and took on his character once more and said, "I'm still down, though."

After months of resisting Metropolitan SDA Junior Academy, my resistance had eventually turned into a reluctant acceptance, and an expectation that meeting new white students would mean they would want to hide pencils in my hair or would ask me why it looks like pubes. I had seen this movie before. The best I could do was pretend that I wasn't bothered, because taking offense would only result in them saying how they were only joking, and the only person who would suffer consequences would be me.

Hearing racist jokes were opportunities to show how much I could take and *not* be offended, so when someone asked, "Two black guys are riding in a car. Who's driving?" I would pretend it didn't matter when they answered, "the police."

When someone else followed, "What's the difference between a Black person and a bucket of shit?" I would pretend it didn't matter when they answered, "the bucket."

When I heard "Why do Black people have white palms?" I would pretend it didn't matter when they answered, "Because everyone's got a *little* good in them."

No one knows more racist jokes than those of us who

went to predominately white schools that were a safe environ-ment for budding racists. I became something of a collector of them, memorizing a new one every few months of casual lunchroom conversations, pretending to laugh, or at least pretending not to be bothered. The best I could do was to tell myself that they weren't talking about me.

But compared with Metropolitan Seventh-day Adventist Junior Academy, Great Lakes Adventist Academy was virtu-ally unimaginable. At Metro, after the final bell and the school day was over, I cleaned the school with Brandi, Precious, and Claudette and went back home to Darryl. GLAA, on the other hand, was its own planet, an isolated community nearly ineffable to a non-Adventist.

Even the name was too awkward to ever share with non-Adventists. It took weeks before I read the full name Great Lakes Adventist Academy and put together that the acronym was meant to sound like "Glah." Until then I had thought it was "glock," like the gun, and I was saying it wrong without anyone noticing.

My new home was made up of four buildings. There was North Hall, which was the boy's dorm, home to 100 pubes-cent boys. South Hall was the girl's dorm. On the east was the school building, standing across from the cafeteria building and attached to a multimillion-dollar recreation facility. In the middle was the quad, or "center campus," a football field sized area that was empty except for three benches. One of the most memorable things about GLAA though wasn't its campus with its four two-story buildings situated around a field. What was memorable were the rules that governed it.

One of the earliest rules I learned at GLAA was the invis-ible line. A paved walkway connected the four buildings of the small campus, and 20 yards in front of each dorm was the invisible line. It was the threshold for the opposite dorm that you couldn't pass.

Boys and girls weren't allowed in each other's dorms for any reason, a transgression which was easily grounds for expulsion, so countless high school sweethearts stood at those lines, facing each other with the crack of the sidewalk dividing them in the middle, talking about their relationships or saying goodnight with an A-framed hug, the only type of physical touch that was allowed. A-frame hugs meant that both people leaned forward to hug, using arms and shoulders so that the two huggers looked like the letter A. They were meant to keep our midsections from touching.

One of the greatest fantasies for students was sneaking into the other dorm, and there was always a token storyteller who knew someone who had, or if they were bold enough liars, said they did it themselves.

Where the invisible line was a small governance that embodied the principles that ruled us, it was our schedule that enforced it. We had a consistent schedule each day, beginning our day with Chapel every morning as a school at 7:15 a.m. School began at 8 a.m. and ended at 3 p.m., followed by your choice of choir, orchestra, gymnastics, or yearbook committee as extracurricular activities. Dinner was at 5:30 p.m., followed by two hours of recreational time that was our only unstructured time of the day.

Recreation was my favorite time of the day when I could play basketball or throw a football with other sports fans, but being an athlete meant something different in an Adventist Academy than it did in regular schools. Sports leagues weren't endorsed, so being a student athlete meant being an intramural star in various seasonal leagues. A student athlete at GLAA couldn't compete with other student athletes, which was commonly an awkward concern when talking with students from other schools. Lucky for us, interaction with the outside world was relatively rare. GLAA was our world, as it was meant to be.

Dorm Worship separated the boys from the girls at 7:15 p.m., and couples and friends said their goodbyes at the invisible lines before turning in for the night. The basement of each dorm had a small chapel where we had an evening worship service each night, led by the dorm's Dean. Mine was Dean Holt, a pious yet intimidating man due to his temper and muscled build. He was an Adventist Dwayne "The Rock" Johnson, handsome, ethnically ambiguous, charming, intimidating, and strong. He led us as we sang hymns and heard one last sermon, given either by Dean Holt himself or one of our schoolmates, and the evening ended with Study Hall, which is when we were closed in our respective bedrooms for the last two hours of each night. Resident assistants checked rooms one by one to account for each student in our rooms, and to make sure that no one was where they weren't allowed. Lights-out and funeral silence began at 10 p.m.

We spent every minute of our lives on that campus, except for home leave, the monthly break where students would be shuttled on buses to their respective parts of the state to be picked up by their parents and see their families for a few days. The idea of leaving campus was otherwise laughable.

In our bubble we grew accustomed to the rules until our prison felt more like home than our actual homes. Jewelry of all kinds was forbidden, including earrings. A boy's hair could be no longer than several inches, judged by the criteria of whether it goes past your eyebrows or was shaggy enough to touch your collar. It was clear that the school was facing new territory with me, as their rules around hair weren't exactly written for Black boys and my braids meant my hair never ever fell into my eyes. White boys joked about the reverse-racism suffered as my hair grew longer and the school administration clearly decided that it wasn't a battle that they were willing to fight. Only one Black boy posed the problem. They would let it slide.

Computers were allowed to upper classmen, but without internet. Meat wasn't allowed on campus, though some would sneak in real beef jerky after home leave. Television and movies weren't allowed and were nowhere to be found. I had to live off the memory of the media I knew by heart.

What would end up getting me in trouble though, was that no music was allowed on campus.

Hymns were okay because the angels were singing with us, but we weren't allowed to have music devices of any kind. We were even banned from singing the songs of certain musicians if those artists were deemed particularly offensive. System of a Down could be heard hummed down the dorm halls as an act of passive rebellion, and if the student was caught, they would do their best to explain that the tune was from a different song. "Aerials" was particularly catchy in 2001 and was specifically banned from being sung.

GLAA enforced its rules through hours of free labor and fines. Break dress code, sing "Aerials," or mouth off to a teacher, and you were served "hours," which was free labor for the school. They were given in blocks of two hours and comprised anything from scrubbing toilets to raking leaves, and you worked off your hours with free labor until your debt was paid.

Back at home, mom and Cliff were left with an empty nest. Both Darryl and I had gone away for school, and without us, I expected Cliff would be happy. But he wasn't.

He wanted us back.

He *needed* us back.

His marriage to my mom had already begun to deteriorate. Without their shared focus on raising Darryl and me, Cliff had lost the most important power he had over my mom. He had already been successful in isolating her from her family and friends. She no longer spoke to grandma regularly, or the rest of our family, after Cliff had convinced her that they were jealous of her and wanted to hurt her. She no longer spoke to Shirley, who had taken us to live in Canada when we were homeless. And Cliff was already making plans to move them out of my mom's house into an apartment in his name.

My mom was friendless and without family, completely dependent on him. But he needed his leverage, lest he be left with a woman who might rediscover herself, who might find out that he was miserable, who might decide she didn't need him. Without us, Cliff didn't have the most important thing he needed that he could save her from. The two boys he had convinced her were horrible.

Darryl was gone and wouldn't return, but he was still looking for his chance at me.

And I gave it to him.

CHAPTER 16

MINORITY SPORT

The first time I was called a nigger with a hard "r" was at GLAA by Austin Wilson. Austin was the local student who was actually *from* Cedar Lake, Michigan, the small town where GLAA was located. He didn't live in the dorms, so I only saw him in school during the day before he was allowed to go home off campus. Austin was a reader and was the only hand that would be raised in English class as Ms. Waters asked questions from the curriculum of white American male writers we were assigned.

We were once assigned to a reading group together in English Literature, and Ms. Waters asked the class to break into small groups around the classroom. Five of us sat in the back corner of the classroom, a small circle where we chatted and wrote notes on our assignment. Part of that assignment was to write a list of hobbies, and I offered basketball.

Under his breath, but loud enough for the group to hear, Austin muttered, "Basketball is a minority sport."

Not angrily, but in the intellectual voice of a young white supremacist who believes their status is of a natural order, provable by science and logic. It was a test, to workshop his racism in the open, to gauge reaction and pushback. It was a test our group failed, because nobody said anything but me.

"What do you mean, a minority sport?" I asked. "White people play basketball. White people *invented* basketball."

"Basketball and football, they're minority sports," he said.

A girl in our group, sensing the tension, steered the conversation back to our work.

I was unsure what to do, this being the first time in my predominately white, token-Black-kid setting that a racist comment came with the sneer of malice. I had heard countless racist jokes, but this felt different. I asked myself if his comment was *racist*-racist, and I assured myself that it wasn't. It wasn't like he called me a slur. Now *that* I would stand up against.

I had some reference points for navigating as the only Black boy, references that were both empowering and dangerous in their scarcity. In a diverse setting, a Black person can be who they are. In a monochrome one, a Black person becomes *The Black Character*, one that is, above all else, an implicit torchbearer for what it means to be Black. In Cedar Lake, Michigan, without Black mentorship or a single Black teacher, I searched for what it meant to be one of the small numbers of Black boys.

Mentally, I flipped through my Encyclopedia of pop culture, consulting each page.

There was Lieutenant Worf of the Starship Enterprise. *Star Trek: The Next Generation* was the first Star Trek I had known, having had no prior exposure to the original series of William Shatner, Leonard Nimoy, Nichelle Nichols, and George Takei. It was the original Star Trek in 1966 that broke barriers for many sci-fi television fans, including an interracial kiss in 1967 between Shatner's Captain Kirk and Filipina Lt. Marlena Moreau, and later an even more high-profile interracial kiss between Kirk and Uhura. While earlier interracial kisses have been discovered on television, both kisses are considered groundbreaking for the culture, and the show's progressiveness was a hit, with creator Gene Roddenberry sharing his commitment to "a liberalism that believed in prosperity, technological progress, and universal humanity" that continued into seven Star Trek spinoff television series.

One of those spinoffs came two decades later in 1987's *Star Trek: The Next Generation*, its title implying the continuation of a legacy of which I was completely unaware. All I knew was Geordi, Guinan, and Worf were Black. The three of them, a trinity in my eyes, had personalities that ranged from Guinan's understated confidence, to Worf's warrior pride, to Geordi being analytical, diminutive, and unromantically involved. But they were three amongst their comrades on the Enterprise. Classes at GLAA had a worse ratio.

Five-to-one was the go-to ratio in popular media. From *Captain Planet* to *Saved by the Bell* to *Mighty Morphin' Power Rangers*.

Power Rangers was one of the more egregious displays of stereotype-based tokenism, with a Black actor, Walter Emanuel Jones, as the Black Ranger, and also an Asian actress, Thuy Trang, as the Yellow Ranger. The Saban Entertainment-produced series rarely missed an opportunity to highlight Zack, the Black Ranger, body rolling and breakdancing before a fight.

Spinoffs adopted the ratio as well. *Tattooed Teenage Alien Fighters from Beverly Hills* was a low-rate copy hoping to emulate the Power Rangers' success and had a Black character named Swinton. *VR Troopers* traded a token Black teammate for a Black home-based father figure in Professor Horatio Hart, the Troopers' equivalent to Zordon. Three main Troopers, two close allies, same five-to-one ratio.

If a token Black character in a white landscape didn't have the answers I needed, maybe I needed to look in Black shows.

Black family shows in the '90s had several unspoken tenets, the primary one being that they had a responsibility to show Black families in a positive light. Despite most characters in the shows being Black, they existed in a white media landscape that made a Black show *itself* the token, rather than its characters. It became *The Black Show*, with all the responsibility of *The Black Character*, just on a macro scale.

Black family sitcoms I grew up on were notably more wholesome than those of the '70s and '80s. The pendulum had swung away from what many had felt were embarrassing portrayals of Black families on television. *Good Times* was about a Black family's struggles being poor, *The Jeffersons* was about a poor Black family getting hit by a bus to become rich, *Sanford and Son* was about a Black family running a junkyard, and *Roc* was the family life of a garbage man.

Legends, all of them, and for good reason. They highlighted the Black experience, paved the way for the continued success of Black-led programming, and made comedy specifically for us. But a change began as the '80s transitioned into the next decade, led by *The Cosby Show*. An era of respectability was taking hold, and the new guard would highlight successful Black families in successful family settings. Families like the Evans in *Good Times* would be replaced with ones like the Huxtables, and shows like *Family Matters*, *The Parent 'Hood*, and *Sister Sister* were born.

They served as "positive Black role models" for those of us Black kids who watched them, a cultural topic de jour of the time that combated violent or clownish media portrayals. "Respectable" versus non-respectable programming lived in a quiet war in the corner of Black culture, unnoticed by most white people.

But "respectable" shows offered something else beneath the surface of their positivity and normalization of Black economic success. It meant successful Black families were depicted in middle to upper-class white American settings. Black families had to navigate white spaces to triumph.

My brain found what it was looking for.

Every Black family-based program would have a slur episode, the one where a member of the family would come in direct contact with racism. The severity of the racism ranged across programs, from a character encountering more subtle discrimination, to the TV family sitcom's nuclear option of having one if its children directly called the slur. Kid's shows did the same, only indirectly, with muties, meatbags, and mudbloods.

White live-action TV shows rarely had a race episode since it would only scare advertisers, and the height of white progressive piety at the time was to not see race at all. But while white families, both onscreen and off, were being taught not to see race, Black TV families were having conversations like "the talk" about police brutality, often using the most pure-hearted character as an example that respectability won't save you.

There was the drugs episode, like in *The Fresh Prince of Bel-Air* where Carlton found drugs in Will's locker and nearly died, or the guns episode where Will was shot and Carlton bought a gun the next day, or the racial profiling episode where Will and Carlton were arrested for driving Uncle Phil's car. Even *Family Matters* would have its slur episode where Laura Winslow had nigger spray painted on her locker, and an episode where Eddie was profiled, and Carl stood up for his son against a white police officer. Any Black TV show would be culturally remiss not to include its voice in the conversations.

I had watched enough of these episodes that I should have been prepared, but I wasn't.

Back at school, my biology class separated us into small groups for labs, and this time Austin and I were thankfully apart. Each group held a station to look into microscopes or run a small test, and the groups rotated from station to station. I worked with a friend in my group named Dan, and as we moved from one station to another, Austin bumped into me.

"Nigger," he whispered.

Time froze as I looked around to see who else had heard it. There was an expectation, a threatened consequence made by young Black boys who spoke confidently on playgrounds and at television screens about the things they would do if someone were to ever call them that. Being called a slur was something that happened in the past, maybe to a grandparent, *but if someone ever said that today*, I had fantasized about what I would do.

Yet there it was, happening that day.

I had been used to racist jokes, made uncomfortable and rendered silent by the lose-lose options of speaking up and risk being made fun of for your sensitivity in a setting where sensitivity is unaccepted, or to be quiet to maintain order and feel a bit of yourself break away, a small piece every time, a cowardice clearing the path to self-hatred.

But the line was being called a racial slur, right? In the hierarchy of insults, there was no higher calling for violent response. *He called you gay. He called your mom a bitch. He called you a nigger.* Those were the sparks of imaginary fights that Detroit Urban had taught me to fight.

"What?" I asked, buying myself time. I was expecting his denial. I was hoping for it.

But he didn't deny it.

He said it again, this time loud enough for a few other students to hear, so I charged toward him to collect his debt, the fulfillment of my duty.

I wasn't sure if I would throw a punch or not, but I was willing. Before I could, though, Dan wrapped his arms around me.

It was the "hold me back" moment from every playground, a boy yelling over a peacemaker to hide his pain, to hide his embarrassment, to hide his tears. A boy pushing towards a fight because that's what we were taught to do. He would have to make a scene to attract more peacemakers to separate him from his abuser, or else he'll have to do what he has to do, what he really doesn't want to do, but what he's willing to do.

Our Biology teacher, Mr. Cousins, waited until we were separated before asking what happened.

"Austin called me a nigger," is what happened, but it was clear that Mr. Cousins was uncomfortable and wanted the situation over as fast as possible.

He directed us to our next microscope stations, and that was the end of that.

A few weeks later I took a hall pass to the bathroom during a particularly boring Government class. When I left the bathroom, I slowly walked the hallway back to the classroom, reading bulletin boards and trying to waste time along the way. Austin Wilson walked the empty hall as well, taking a break from his own class, and we both stopped at the dual water fountains.

We bent over the fountains to drink, where he whispered it in my ear.

"Nigger."

But I was relieved.

I didn't have to yell, or fight, or get myself into any more trouble than I'd already found when dealing with white kids.

Nobody was watching, so I pretended it didn't happen.

I went back to class.

CHAPTER 17

WHITE POWER

My earliest friends at GLAA had been three white kids I met after moving into the dorm, Alex Mason, Alex Jordan, and Jordan Marshall. It quickly became clear that Alex Jordan was more befitting to another crowd of the dude-bro variety, and he would eventually make that social transition. But he would still hang out with Alex Mason occasionally, who seemed to tolerate him well enough despite slowly recognizing, as the rest of us did, that even for our age Alex Jordan was something of a moron.

Alex Mason and I bonded over both basketball and rap, him being a tamer version of what I saw in Kyle. He was a pastor's kid like Mike, with the same humor and interests, along with the same intellectual curiosity that lived beneath the surface of their childish teen exteriors. Alex, too, probably got straight A's or something close to it. We spent time in each other's dorm rooms often.

Each dorm room at GLAA had a carpeted floor, two beds that could be bunked or separated, two desks, two closets on opposite ends, and a large counter in between them with a large, wide mirror in the center. There were four group bathrooms, one for each grade level, with three shower stalls each for us to take shifts each morning. With its rules and structure, the dorm culture felt something of a cross between the military and prison.

There was a countdown to daily room check each morning that was announced on the PA system, one of several announcements I grew accustomed to hearing blasted through the hallway speakers before Dean Holt would quickly tap his master key twice on each doorknob before pushing the door open over the rough carpet and grading each room on a scale of one to five. Scoring a three or above meant that you passed, scoring below three meant that you failed, and failing more than once in a week meant you were added to the list of students who would lose their recreational time.

I grew accustomed to the rhythm of dorm life. The countdowns, the announcements, the two taps of the key against the doorknob before my door was unlocked and rustled against the rough carpet as it opened, and Dean Holt would walk in with a Randall Weems-like resident assistant holding a clipboard.

"Four," Dean Holt would say, before I'd hear him shut the door behind him and move onto the next room, where I would hear it again, only fainter this time, the sound of two taps, the door rustling over the rough carpet, "two," the door closing, and then another two taps, fainter still. We could measure distance by the sound of those two taps, knowing whether Dean Holt or an RA were three doors away, two, or right next door.

Announcements had their own format that also became normal, starting with a loud beep over the hallway speakers, followed by a front desk worker repeating the announcement two and a half times. No matter what was happening, joking, wrestling or masturbating, time would stop at the sound of the beep as we listened through our doors or stuck our heads out if we were expecting a phone call.

"Room check in five minutes, room check in five minutes, room check," or "Jordan Calhoun, you have a phone call in the lobby, Jordan Calhoun, you have a phone call in the lobby, Jordan Calhoun," or "Lights out in 10 minutes, lights out in 10 minutes, lights out."

Given our concentration in a small, two-story dorm, news would spread if someone was known to have contraband like beef jerky or new music from the outside world, or if someone had been caught with them. I learned about shakedowns and lockdowns through the dorm lore passed down through the years by boys living in the boys dorm, like how someone had a cigarette hidden in their room once, causing a shakedown that would sequester every student into the basement chapel as the Deans searched each room from top to bottom. We would gossip about our own hiding strategies, about how we would game the system by hiding our CD player inside the cushion of a couch or inside a bag of corn flakes, or balanced atop the inner ledge of the closet doorframe where you'd have to blindly reach up to find it. Those stories were followed by more dorm lore about the time someone did exactly that and was still caught, and about someone who did the same, was never caught, and became a legend.

I sat next to Alex Mason during my first lockdown. After hearing stories about these kinds of events, I wouldn't have guessed that I would ever be at the center of one. But I hadn't planned on being on the receiving end of a hate crime either.

One afternoon after recreation time, I came back to my dorm room to find "white power" written on the large mirror

191

above the sink. My initial thought was that it was a joke. I felt that the worst thing I could do as one of the few Black students was to take a dorm prank too seriously, but I only grew more worried after I asked the friends on my hall if they'd done it, and everyone gathered around the large mirror and assured me that they hadn't. A few suggested I tell Dean Holt, and reluctantly, I did.

We found ourselves crowded in the small, windowless basement chapel that night, all one hundred of us, after what would have normally been lights out. Dean Holt had seen the mirror, and given his size, anger, and the extent we feared him, we sat reverently. He told us why we were there, that he'd seen something so infuriating, so disgusting, that he would rather have seen anything else. He told us how disappointed he was that something like this could happen. And he told us we wouldn't leave until someone confessed.

Despite being off duty that day, Dean Walsh, the secondary Dean, came from his off-campus housing to stare at us along with Dean Holt in the small basement chapel. Resident assistants joined them on the small, elevated podium looking out at the rest of us who sat uncomfortably in close-quartered pews. After Dean Holt's speech, we sat mostly in silence for the first hour.

By the second hour, upper classmen had begun to take it on themselves to give motivational speeches to encourage whoever had done it to come forward and confess.

By the third hour, tempers flared as students lashed out at one another, especially those who had to work 5 a.m. shifts at the cafeteria. And I sat as quietly as possible, the unwitting center of it all.

A suggestion was made to allow for an anonymous confession, so Dean Holt sent an RA for paper and pencils.

After the RA's tore the paper into halves, each of us was handed a slip of paper and a pen for our anonymous confession, or to offer whatever information we knew to name the person responsible, or to say that we didn't know anything. If the person confessed or was discovered, we could leave and our torment would end, but after the papers were collected and reviewed by Dean Holt in silence, there was a collective outburst when he stood and told us we weren't going anywhere.

Half an hour later, we were given paper again for another chance at anonymous confessions or snitching, and Dean Holt said they had enough information to let us go for the night. There were sighs of relief mixed with grumbles of frustration at whoever wrote the racist taunt, whoever was selfish enough to allow the entire dorm to be held captive for hours, whoever would then confess after forcing everyone to wait that long. More than anything though was the gossip over who it was and whether Dean Holt actually knew or was faking it, either to make the suspects sweat, or because they couldn't keep us there forever and there was no real endgame if the culprit were to wait it out and keep quiet.

News had spread to the girls and the rest of school faculty by the next day, making me one of the worse kinds of celebrities, known for being the victim. I felt embarrassed, knowing that the added kindness and attention from teachers wasn't from anything that I did, but because of what was done to me. We knew that word would spread instantly once the person was caught, that we would see them pack their bags and take a walk of shame if they were expelled, but instead we found ourselves back in the basement chapel that evening for a second day of lockdown.

Either the information didn't pan out, or Dean Holt had

been bluffing to call an end to the first night. Anger simmered from the start this time as we funneled back into our pews. Eyes rolled. Speeches began. Alex Mason angrily bounced his leg down the pew from me as students alternated between passionate adaptations of Martin Luther King quotes, to pleas for consideration of their fellow students who had to suffer alongside them, to promises that there would be no hard feelings if they confessed.

It was a battle of stubbornness with Dean Holt, a game of chicken that Dean Holt couldn't win if the racist asshole just chose to remain an anonymous racist asshole and bided his time. Eventually Dean Holt would have to give up, or parents would get involved or something would happen for academy life to continue beyond the purgatory of 100 boys being subject to sleep deprivation in a basement cellar on wooden pews.

I was lost in that thought and looking down at the ground when a speech was interrupted by a roar of applause. I looked up to see what had happened, and saw Alex Mason standing down the pew, crying.

My confusion gave way to understanding. It had been Alex who wrote "white power" on my mirror, but being a grade below me, he lived down a different hallway and had missed the original commotion from when I was asking if it was a joke. He only learned I'd seen it after Dean Holt was involved, after we were pulled into lockdown.

His shaking hadn't been from anger. His red eyes hadn't been from being tired. He was terrified after his racist prank had gone wrong in a way that anyone but a teenage white kid from suburban Michigan could have foreseen.

The applause was deafening, and time slowed as he stood red-faced and crying, wiping his eyes and mouthing "I'm sorry."

It was a moment from a Very Special Episode of '90s television, or from *Remember the Titans* that had come out that very year, the kind where the Black person would forgive racism, where there would be a grand gesture of that forgiveness, a climax moment of conciliation, one small step for a man, one giant leap for mankind.

I had a role to play, and so I played it.

I stood up and hugged Alex to the applause of the room, giving them their moment, their public display of forgiveness.

After we were dismissed and Alex Mason had had a private conversation with Dean Holt to discuss what would happen to him, I learned the broader story of what had happened the day "white power" was written in capital letters across my large dorm room mirror.

Alex Mason hadn't been alone. He and Alex Jordan were together when they came up with the idea to use a bar of soap to write "white power" as a joke. When the lockdown began, Alex Mason wanted to confess, but Alex Jordan urged him to stay quiet, that they wouldn't be caught if they just held out.

And he was right, only Alex Mason was sick with guilt until he stood up crying in a room full of people.

The funny pastor's kid, my first friend in boarding school, it was hard not to feel that Alex Mason fit into a growing line of white people who were, at the end of the day, white enough not to be trusted. White like Kyle, who would confess to Mr. Newman that it was him playing DMX only to make the point that he wouldn't suffer consequences. White like Jessica or Amy who wouldn't stick their neck out for me, who would stay quiet, or who weren't sure what they heard. White like Alex Jordan, who wrote "white power" on my mirror and would never confess, not even privately to me.

But Alex Mason stood up, eventually.

There was no evidence against him, no case to be made, only the guilt, something I was familiar with.

Alex Mason was given 25-20, the highest punishment GLAA had to offer outside of expulsion, and he took the embarrassment along with the phone calls to his parents. He became the first white person I knew who in a way stood up for me, and my racial Stockholm Syndrome thanked him, because he could have sat back and got away with it. It meant something to a kid who had only known white people to value him about as little as Alex Jordan did.

A phone call from Dean Holt would explain what happened to my mom and Cliff. The situation was almost enough for Cliff to convince my mom to pull me out of the school, but I didn't want to be at home without Darryl, so I convinced her to let me stay. GLAA was a prison, but Cliff had already started showing signs of being his worst self, and prison was better than that.

He would get his chance a few weeks later.

Before arriving at GLAA, I had packed my CD binder with over 50 albums I had collected from subscriptions to Columbia House. I didn't know they were banned before I arrived, but when I found out they were, I hid them instead of turning them in. But my CDs weren't found in a room search or shakedown. I was tricked into giving them up voluntarily.

Dean Holt had summoned me into his office, having suspected that I had music, and pretended he already knew. He asked me to go get them, and I was too afraid to be caught in a lie, so I walked down the hall to my dorm room and pulled my CD case from its hiding place, balanced on the ledge inside the top of my closet, and brought them to his office. All of them.

At a fine of five dollars per violation, the punishment for my CDs was over $250. In reality, the fine would have been reduced, even eliminated altogether in exchange for hours, if my mom or Cliff were willing to advocate for it, but the money wasn't really the point. Cliff had been looking for his chance to pull me out of boarding school and stop wasting his money on tuition, and I gave him the excuse he needed. It was enough for him to use as an example that I was too out of control, even for boarding school, and that I needed to be home with them.

He drove north that same day, a four-hour drive to pull me from school in the middle of a semester. I cried as I packed my room, embarrassed as friends helped take down posters and load boxes, and students gathered to ask what was going on. I was back at home that same day.

I cried for weeks to my mom about wanting to go back. I hadn't wanted to change schools in the first place, but now that I had, the thought of starting over in another school felt like it would destroy me.

I forfeited all my academic credits for the semester.

The rumor would be that I had been expelled.

After Darryl left for college and I was brought back from GLAA, I was the sole child at the whims of Cliff's decision making and my mom's acquiescence to his demands. It was my first time dealing with Cliff without Darryl. Before, we had found humor in laughing at his rants and his hatred. When Darryl and I had been together, Cliff's eccentricities could be funny. Anything could be funny. Laughter was our coping mechanism after dealing with divorce, and homelessness, and not being allowed to see our dad. Even my culture shock of transferring from an all-Black school to an all-white one, and of finding revelations of how different white people were from us, could be funny. Cliff's anger itself could be funny. And when it wasn't funny, Darryl proved that he could stand up to him.

But it wasn't the same after Darryl had left.

By myself, with my older brother having started college, I tried my best not to hyperventilate as I cried.

"You whine like a mule," I told myself. "You are still alive."

"You whine like a mule. You are still alive."

"You whine like a mule. You are still alive."

But it didn't work without him.

Cliff said that although they had pulled me out of school, I still owed them for the fine, and I would pay it off by working for him. He wanted me to go back with him selling Bibles and books door to door.

But if Darryl could stand up to him, I could, too. Even if my voice was shaking.

It wasn't a full-on rant like Darryl's had been. I didn't have the temper or fortitude to yell, or slam on the table, or walk through the house banging on walls. I wouldn't highlight Cliff's abuses or their consequences for me, that I had been pulled from school *twice*, made to transfer *twice*, lost my credits *twice*. I wouldn't tell him how I had tried so hard to get these white people to see me for who I was, or that now there was another false rumor that I had been expelled. I wouldn't say that I had lost my Black friends and that I never really had any white ones. I wouldn't yell that maybe, just maybe, if this was what it took to be a good Christian then maybe it was all a line of *bullshit*. I didn't tell him that at Metro, or at GLAA, or at home, it didn't matter what I did or who I was, I'd just be Black kid, regarded as nothing more than another lazy, stupid, good for nothing, worthless, embarrassment-to-your-race nigger with braids and tattoos.

I wouldn't say all that, like Darryl would have.

Darryl was Bruce Lee. He was Goliath, and Optimus, and Azeem the Great One. He was whatever Saiyan he wanted. But I could at least muster a small defiance.

I just told him I wouldn't sell books for him anymore.

And later one night I woke up to him standing over my bed. The lights were off, and the room was dark, but there he was, a dark silhouette in a dark room.

He stood over the foot of my bed, his fists clenched, and I was too scared to move because I knew he was in control and that there was no escape, except to wake up from a dream. And I so desperately wished it to be a dream.

"You think you're bad, don't you?" he said.

He repeated it over and over, drunk with anger. He said how Darryl thought he was tough, how I must think I'm so tough as well. He said how I was screwing things up, and how I was ruining my mom's life. He said all the things he had wanted to say to Darry, that he had wanted to say to his own dad.

And as I laid quietly, looking up at him in the dark, I knew he would never love me.

CHAPTER 18

GOOD FOR NOTHING

I still tried to make a family of the group I had. My exposure to white families exacerbated my desire for the "real" families I saw on TV. Those families were close, spent time together, and cared about each other openly in a way I had never experienced. Aside from church and evening worship, I didn't spend time talking with either of my parents or my stepfather about life. They didn't know my friends' names, or the classes I took in school. I had spent time with Darryl and Deshawn, and that was about it. Adults and kids had separate lives.

One day, I was inspired to change that. What we needed was a catalyst to show how nice a real family could be. I decided I would cook and invite my mom and Cliff for a family dinner. We would talk over dinner, on a regular weekday, just us. We would get to know each other, quip, and gossip like the Winslows, Huxtables, Tanners, and Camdens.

I got started and spent the afternoon in our kitchen making spaghetti, garlic bread, and broccoli. When I was done, I set the table with three place settings. I put napkins under forks and added ice to glasses. And then I called out that it's dinner time, like I'd seen on countless sitcoms and commercials.

After waiting a few minutes, I called again. And then I went upstairs and knocked on my mom and Cliff's door.

"I'm impressed," my mom called down after hearing from Cliff that I made dinner. And for that moment, I knew everything would go as planned. "Can you send up a plate?" she asked.

"You have to come downstairs," I responded. "We can eat together."

I heard steps coming down the stairs. It was Cliff, who told me he had come down to make a plate for my mother.

"Do you want some spaghetti with that sauce?" he asked as he served the pasta onto two plates, one for him and another for my mom.

He let me know I had added too much pasta sauce, and then he walked back upstairs.

After he went upstairs, I sat at the table alone for a few minutes, in case they would change their mind and see the work I'd done making a family dinner. If they just saw that, they would sit with me at the dinner table and we'd have a family dinner. After a few minutes, I took my plate and went into my bedroom to eat on my own and watch TV.

I was enrolled in another Seventh-day Adventist School after being pulled from GLAA after less than one semester. It seemed that mom and Cliff alternated priorities between wanting me to have an Adventist education and not wanting to pay for it, but they chose to send me to a school called Oakwood that was in Taylor, Michigan, another suburb of Detroit. It was another Junior Academy, this one topping out at tenth grade, so it would only be a stop-gap solution until

I finished the rest of the school year when I would need to transfer yet again for my last two years of school.

Oakwood itself wasn't bad. It was a small school like Metro but far more diverse, and I shared the classroom with several other students of color, including my paternal cousin, Grace, who helped soften the rough landing, if only a little bit. Our homeroom teacher, Mr. Buford, was a younger white man who was charismatic and athletic. I liked him, and I developed a crush on an Indonesian girl named Leah, and the freedom from GLAA's draconian rules was nice. I was a little older now and a lot taller. Leah would become my girlfriend for a while, and I made new friends faster than I had at Metro. I even started seeing my dad a bit more. Even though he lived nearby our house, my mom hadn't allowed me to see much of him since that night in the parking lot and the incident with the police, just before I was leaving for the GLAA boarding school.

But any joy I found in my new school in Oakwood was taken away whenever I went home.

Cliff had been sterner than ever after bringing me back home from GLAA, and he seemed especially threatened by my dad's renewed presence. He made a point of criticizing my dad to me often, saying how Darryl and I had learned a lot of bad habits from him, everything from how Darryl drove a car to how much peanut butter we put on our bread. But however much Cliff hated my dad, my dad hated Cliff even more. Dad had heard enough stories from Darryl and me to put together a picture of the man who was raising his sons, and when Cliff picked me up from dad's house one day, I almost expected a fight from my otherwise jovial, nonviolent dad. Cliff was especially demure though when he met my dad, the same way he was when Darryl came home to visit.

I was still small, so he saved his boldness for me.

One day, I was home alone when the phone rang. Expecting it to be my friend Mike from Metro, I went to answer it, but the caller had already hung up. We had one caller ID in our house, which was upstairs in my mom and Cliff's bedroom, where I wasn't allowed to go since they got married because Cliff believed that kids shouldn't be allowed in their parents' rooms. He would set traps to make sure I hadn't gone up there, like placing a small piece of Scotch tape on the bottom corner of the door and the doorjamb to see if the door had been opened while he was gone. The traps were obvious and easy to circumvent, but I rarely bothered. Except in this case, when I felt the teen desperation to know if it was a friend who had called.

I opened the door and ran upstairs, checking the caller ID. It wasn't for me, some number I didn't recognize, and just then I heard the car door shut outside. I sprinted to the stairs and ran down as fast as I could, my steps thumping loudly. I leapt over the last few stairs, only to land with a thud as Cliff and my mom had walked in the doorway.

They were looking straight at me.

"I *knew* it," he started. "You've been watching TV in our room."

I had never watched TV in their room, but since buying a big-screen TV Cliff had been convinced that I was secretly sneaking into their room to watch it. The accusation caught me off guard. I knew I was guilty, but I was guilty of going upstairs to check the caller ID, not to sneak a chance to watch television in their bedroom.

He stormed upstairs to look for evidence, and to my surprise, he found what he wanted. The TV had been set to a channel he didn't watch. In fact, he said it was a channel he *never* watched.

I continued to plead my case, telling him that it wasn't me who had changed the channel, that I just gone upstairs to check the caller ID. When he asked how I could explain the channel, I looked to my mom. If I hadn't watched it, and Cliff claimed to never watch the channel as well, it must have been *her* who had been watching the TV most recently. She watched TV all the time. If Cliff were wrong, she could solve the whole thing by saying that it was a channel she had been watching.

In this small way, she could rescue me.

If the demon was walking toward her son, she could step in front of it. She could protect me.

I looked at her desperately, telling her, without words, that I knew it was her, and that all she needed to do was say so. *Aren't you going to say it*? I begged with my eyes. *Aren't you?*

When she looked down, I realized she wouldn't. I was alone. Not just in the moment, but a meaningful alone. My mom's loyalty was to him, to protect her marriage and save herself from the exhaustion of interceding on my behalf and facing a tirade turned towards her instead of me. She was his, Darryl was away in college, and it was just me.

Days later, Cliff was driving me to school, still seething over his estimations of my misbehavior and obstinacy. His rants would wander across topics, like a stream-of-consciousness thread of grievances that connected one subject to another. He was still resentful that I was costing him money and that I wouldn't sell books for him to pay him back.

As we drove, he ranted on with his characterizations of each race. He said how white people had no morals and would have sex with animals. He was also angry at Black people, embracing the view that our failures to carry ourselves a certain way were the reason for the poverty he saw around him. He hated the poor, "ghetto" Black people who filled Detroit. If we would abandon meat, live by God's law, and take care of ourselves, we wouldn't have to live like this. If we lived like him, we would all be better.

I sat silently through his filibuster, knowing that a response would only provoke him to carry on longer. My silence only provoked him further, until he said, "Black people are lazy, ignorant, and good for nothing. You're a perfect example of that."

I didn't gasp. I didn't roll my eyes or contest this statement. In that moment, I had one clear, distinct thought. It felt calm and logical, almost euphoric, like solving a math equation where everything suddenly worked.

I could jerk the steering wheel into oncoming traffic and kill us both.

The only thing that saved me from what felt like a calm, rational decision was the fleeting thought that I would also kill whoever was driving in the oncoming vehicle. Had there been a tree instead, I would most likely have done it.

When I arrived at school I got out of the car, slammed the door behind me, and walked inside. When I got home, my mom told me that I owed Cliff an apology. Apparently, he was upset that I had left rudely, without saying goodbye.

CHAPTER 19

REPRESENT

Since Oakwood ended at the tenth grade, we had to decide where I would attend school for eleventh and twelfth grades. I began my campaign early, because I wanted to go back to GLAA. I didn't care if I was banned from watching movies, listening to music, having a phone, or using the Internet. I didn't care if there was worship twice a day, or room checks, or racist jokes. Anything was better than being left alone with mom and Cliff.

It was the Holy Spirit who started me on this path to begin with, and I decided it was the Holy Spirit who would get me back. I told my mom about the church services and dorm worships and how much I enjoyed them. I lied about the school's teachers having a strong impression on me, that they nurtured my mind and my soul. I told her that going to boarding school was best for my walk with God. I told her that the Holy Spirit had impressed on *my* heart that I was meant to be there. I told a dozen lies, and then lied about how much those lies meant to me in a letter that I typed out to her, summarizing why she needed to send me back. And it worked.

To start my junior year of high school, I was on my way back to middle-of-nowhere Michigan. I could live with whatever GLAA threw at me. Anything but home.

Since I had lost a semester of credits, I would have to either take double the classes to graduate with a college preparatory degree, or graduate with fewer credits to earn a GED. I chose to take double the classes, partly because I didn't want to graduate with a GED diploma and be stigmatized as being lesser than my white peers, but also because I wanted to prove to them, and especially to Cliff, that I could.

I was angry and motivated, and I was growing more stubborn as I got older. My confidence grew from feeling I had nothing to lose. What could anyone take from me? I didn't have a family, or close friends, or movies. I'd been homeless and fatherless and friendless at different points in my life. I had been told I was worthless. My peers at GLAA thought I had been expelled. Even my faith in God had begun to fracture as I wrote the letter to my mom and realized that I was lying to her not just about GLAA, but also about some of my beliefs I was starting to question. Why not prove everyone wrong? Why not be the character with stubborn pride? Or a heart of gold? Or a code of ethics? I'd seen it before. I knew what it looked like. For starters, I could take extra classes each semester because nothing could stop me.

Returning to the dorm at GLAA, I started to attract friends based on a decision I'd made back home the previous summer. I had saved some of the money I had earned from working at Taco Bell to buy a foosball table from Sports Authority, a large sporting goods store that sat in the plaza next door to the Super K-Mart where Darryl had worked.

Often while Darryl worked that summer, I would spend hours roaming the plaza during his full eight-hour shift in the deli department, wandering back and forth between Super K-Mart and Sports Authority. I knew their aisles by heart and I imagined, department by department, what I would buy if I had the money.

Back at Metro I had explored Sports Authority in an attempt to get into hobbies that were popular with the white kids in Michigan who grew up near lakes. I had decided that my thing would be fishing, based on one of my fondest memories from when I felt most like part of a family.

I had been in middle school when Darryl, our mom, and I were visiting my grandma after she moved to North Carolina to live with my aunt, uncle, and cousins. We were invited by an older local couple to go fishing, and my aunt and uncle took them up on the offer. My family in North Carolina lived like a *real* family, like the kind I wanted. Theirs was a five-bedroom house with a grandma, two parents, and two kids. We drove out to the woods and hiked through the lake on a beautiful day, our fishing gear in tow, until we found their small lake.

Darryl and I were city kids who didn't even know how to bait our hooks, so expectations were modest as we fiddled with worms and were given instructions. What happened next became Calhoun family legend. I caught my first fish, a largemouth bass. Then Darryl caught his. Then a second, and a third. We caught fish after fish, over a dozen between the two of us, yelling "Represent" across the lake to each other after each one. Nas' album *Illmatic* had come out and our song was "Represent," prompting what became our mantra of yelling it over and over.

The family who had invited us fishing had never seen that big a catch in a single day, and the Calhoun boys became known as the kids who "represent." When we got back home to my aunt and uncle's house, grandma hugged me as the family regaled her with stories of what had happened, how we boys had represented, and how we had come home with buckets of fish. Grandma took those buckets and fried the fish for dinner, and we sat around a dining room table, my mom, Darryl, aunt, uncle, cousins, grandma, and me, and retold the stories over and over again.

When I found myself surrounded by white kids who went wakeboarding with their family in the summer and ice skating in the winter, I knew I had fishing, so when I learned that Metro would take us on a class trip to Maine, I was excited. I would loiter in the fishing section of Sports Authority, subscribe to Cabela's catalog, and save money for a fishing rod and tackle box. I had all this fishing gear in my bedroom in our small house with no access to water, but Maine would be my chance. I decided I would represent by out-fishing a classmate named Chet Hansen, who was popular for being good at fishing in the way that only an affluent white kid in Michigan could be. But I'd catch more than him. He would lose to the Black kid from the city, and I would represent. But as we spent hours on a large multilevel boat off the coast of Maine, Chet caught a fish first. Then he caught a second. Then a third. He caught fish after fish, and I had caught nothing. I was holding back my tears just fine until he ended the day by catching a record-breaking walleye for the state of Maine. That's the shit that broke me. That fucking walleye, man. They were taking pictures and shit. Measuring it out. I had no fucking idea what I was doing.

Chet's record-breaking walleye was why I skipped the outdoor sports aisle at Sports Authority the summer before GLAA and bought a foosball table instead. A store clerk had taken pity on me after seeing me browse the store day after day and told me I could take the floor model for half off. I spent $150 on that foosball table, suffered Cliff's complaints of my wasting money on something so stupid, and arrived back at GLAA with the most fun room in the dorm.

Jordan Michael Marshall became my roommate, one of the friends I had met the previous year. Our similarities lent themselves to our bonding. We had the same first and middle names, we were both younger siblings to a brother three years older than us, we were both born on the 21st, one month apart. Our chance similarities made for the type of high school friendship that felt destined. Jordan seemed effortless in who he was, a sincere, humble kid disinterested in being popular, or excelling in school, or proving himself to anybody. He simply existed, ego-less and carefree. If he used media to inform his identity of who he was or would become, he had so many options that his amalgamation of archetypes allowed him to be truly original, his unassuming, rural Michigan, goodhearted self. I didn't resent him for it but envied the ease with which he seemed to navigate the world knowing who he was and being good with it.

I made other important friends, like David Fayed and Carlos Garcia. David was Egyptian, Carlos was Puerto Rican, and the two lived down the hall as roommates in whom I saw a similar journey to mine. Both would be instrumental to my life in separate ways, but Carlos would be first.

Carlos had been raised Seventh-day Adventist, but it didn't take long before I realized he wasn't like the rest of the students at places like Metro or GLAA. His dad was a Puerto Rican New Yorker, and Carlos had bounced around as a kid across predominately white spaces and non-white ones. We would swap stories of New York and Detroit, the types of stories we wouldn't share with our other peers because they didn't have to grow up as fast as we did. Where I admired

Jordan Marshall for the ease of his whiteness, I started to admire Carlos more for gripping tight to who he was, for facing the challenges that came with being a brown-skinned Puerto Rican, and for the resilience he built from it. Carlos had so much pride that it was infectious, and when I was with him, I couldn't help but feel pride in my strength, too.

One day, I was in Carlos' dorm room when a white student wandered in to join us. Carlos had been talking about Felix Trinidad, a pro boxer with six world titles who was considered the greatest Puerto Rican boxer of all time. Carlos loved Trinidad, and he and I bonded over Jay-Z's "Lyrical Exercise" that had woven the Puerto Rican icon's name into a verse. When the white kid said that he hadn't heard of Felix Trinidad, and that no one had heard of him, Carlos didn't hesitate.

"No, *you* don't know who he is," Carlos said. "Because you're fucking *stupid*. And your only hope in life is that I'm just as *stupid* as you are. But I'm not. I'm *smarter* than you. *That's* why you don't know who Felix Trinidad is. Now get the fuck out of my room."

And Carlos was right. He *was* smarter than him. He was smarter than most everyone I knew. Every student had a campus job that ranged from factory worker to teacher's assistant, and Carlos' job was working in the computer lab after he taught himself networking. When I found out Carlos was a nerd, we would spend hours talking about things like video games and anime, until he figured out how to connect his dorm computer to the internet in the administration building and we spent hours secretly playing *X-Men vs Street Fighter II* in the only dorm room in the school with internet. When he told me that his favorite *Dragon Ball Z* moment was when Gohan yelled "I've had enough of you Frieza," I knew

I had found a friend for life. We played basketball together, quoted movies together, and we would stand up to anyone who crossed us together.

Carlos wasn't with me back at home, but if I was lucky, Darryl was. Cliff had been successful in moving himself and my mom out of 6841 Rutland, the house she had bought, and into a quiet suburban neighborhood on Belleville Lake, a 30-minute drive west of Detroit. He moved away from the poor Black people he hated and into a ground floor condo. The lake was right outside the door, as I learned when I came to our new home during our monthly school break. It looked like something from *Dawson's Creek*. Nicer than the lake, though, was that Darryl was there with me. He was on break from school too, and a renewed infatuation with Sylvester Stallone's *Rocky* had us going on runs at night to explore our new neighborhood and coming home each night to watch the next installment of the series.

By the time we got to *Rocky III*, Cliff had enough.

We didn't have furniture in our new place yet, so Darryl and I were laying on the carpet when Cliff approached behind us.

"You should be embarrassed for watching that," he said.

When we ignored him, he got angrier. He said how the movie was unrealistic. He said we should be ashamed of ourselves watching a white fighter beat a Black fighter. He said how he'd never watch a movie like that. He was trying to provoke us, but it wasn't working as we offered short answers to pacify him. That was the plan. Wait it out until he went back to his bedroom where our mom quietly watched TV, rewind what we missed, and continue our night. Or so I thought.

"You're lying," Darryl said.

Cliff said how he'd never watch a Rocky movie, but we

knew that he had. It was a white lie only meant to enable his criticism, and a silly one at that. *Of course* he had seen Rocky. We'd heard him quote it before, only he thought we had never noticed.

"You really think we believe that?" Darryl asked.

That white lie was the spark that began the fire. Cliff was indignant about being called a liar and got the confrontation he had provoked. He'd been waiting to put Darryl back in his place since the day Darryl slammed on the table and banged on the walls at 6841 Rutland. This was the rematch he wanted, and he told us why he had to wait.

"This ain't your mama's house anymore, boy," he said. "That last time, I was at your *mama's* house." He said *mama* with emphasis, as if my mom's house disgusted him, a barrier to his patriarchy, a barrier he had finally overcome. "But this is *my* house," he said through gritted teeth, pointing at his chest. "*Mine.* You can't talk to me like that."

But Darryl felt he could, so Darryl stood up.

When Darryl started to speak, Cliff stepped forward to his face.

Cliff was different from the man he had pretended to be when he and my mom first met. He was different from the man he had pretended to be in church or selling Bibles. He was even different from the man who had criticized us, made us run, called us lazy. Those were tempered versions of Cliff, the ones that suppressed the worst of what was inside him. But what we saw now was who Cliff really was, and now that we were in *his* house, he could finally change to be himself. This was his final form.

But I wasn't the same anymore, either. When Cliff stepped forward to Darryl's face, I did what I'd seen my big brother do.

I stood up, too.

We both stood in Cliff's face as he called us ungrateful. He called us disrespectful. He called us arrogant. We stood there anyway, big brother and little brother, as defiant as we wanted.

Then he stopped, but it wasn't us who stopped him.

"Don't talk to them like that."

My mom had come out from her room, and for the first time I saw her stand up to him. Our fight with Cliff had become her fight with Cliff, and the two of them argued through the living room, and the kitchen, and the hallway. My mom fought him about how he spoke to us. She fought about how he treated us. She fought about how he treated her. Darryl and I joined in too, in a cathartic address of his abuses.

Darryl fought with him.

I fought with him.

My mom fought with him.

She told him to get out, that she'd had enough.

"This is *mine* now! It's *my* name on the papers!" he yelled.

"Fine," my mom said. "Then *we'll* leave."

And we did.

In the short term we stayed with a family friend, but I would go back to boarding school and Darryl back to college, and my mom would find her own apartment closer to the city that we had left behind. She would live alone, without her children and without the man she had become dependent on.

My mom had finally stood up to him. She stood up for Darryl. She stood up for *me*. I felt strong in seeing my mother be strong. I felt strong in seeing my brother be strong. I felt strong in seeing myself be strong. And I *never* saw Cliff again.

CHAPTER 20

SEX EDUCATION, CONTINUED

My mom and Cliff divorced while I was busy at GLAA, pushing through extra classes to make up for the credits I had lost. In a movie, my troubles would have ended with the expulsion of Cliff from my life, but it wasn't a movie. I was still finding myself through high school and figuring out my religious beliefs. How many of them were a means to justify the church's rules, or GLAA's rules, or my mom's decisions? How much was fear of the outside world? What was so scary about Halloween, or Pokémon, or Harry Potter?

GLAA issued "hours" of free labor and charged fines to keep me in line where fear couldn't, and the fear was beginning to lose its grip, including sexually. Having sex at GLAA meant expulsion if a student was found out, but that wouldn't stop me from pushing boundaries from lingering hugs to hidden handholds. I grew more brazen as I grew more comfortable with the campus, finding the areas of campus where faculty and staff could scarcely keep an eye on us, places like stairwells, buses, and bathrooms. I learned each place without a camera and each event without a chaperone.

Sexual activity carried a different risk than hours or fines. Being caught holding hands or making out would land you on something called "social holiday," or "social" for short, which meant you weren't allowed to speak with the person you were caught with for seven days. Two people on social weren't allowed to sit together, work together, or otherwise be together until their social holiday was over, and to enforce the separation, each teacher, pastor, administrator, and dean knew the status of any students on the list. If a couple on social was caught breaking it, their social period would be doubled, though I never knew this to happen. Instead, couples would count down the days, communicating by messages passed through mutual friends.

Outside of school hours, staff rotated supervision responsibilities, so our sexual freedoms depended on who was on duty. Mrs. Jenkins on duty meant center campus would be open and we could be outside, Dean Holt on duty meant we were locked in our dorm, a wild card like Pastor Culver meant all bets were off because he gave Bible studies and was oblivious to everything happening around him.

But studying the Bible *did* help to keep us busy. Bible class was where we studied prophesy and our Adventist beliefs, because the most important skill of an Adventist was knowing the Word of God. Bible stories were easy for me after a childhood of *Egypt to Canaan* and *The Greatest Adventures: Stories from the Bible*, but understanding prophesy was the gold standard of Biblical knowledge, and it was a lot harder. The most important prophesies came from the books of Daniel and Revelation, two books of the Bible so confusing that unless you had an Adventist teacher guiding you through them, they would read like the ramblings of Skinny Pete and Badger from *Breaking Bad*. There were seven seals to be opened, three-headed leopards carrying a seductress, a winged lion, and a dragon with horns. There was King Nebuchadnezzar's dream, seven letters to seven churches, and proof of God's true and chosen church. Each detail was a coded message to be cyphered.

I had become less interested in breaking that code though, and more interested in making out in the stairwell with my on-and-off girlfriend, Raven. She was one of the few Black girls in the school, and our dating felt inevitable in the sense that we were two Black kids of the opposite sex in a sea of mostly white students. We were "equally yoked," a term that I had learned meant any number of things depending on who interpreted it, ranging from two people needing to be of the same denomination, to the belief that both partners should be of the same intelligence, status, wealth, or race.

"Do not be unequally yoked with unbelievers," said 2 Corinthians 2:14. "For what partnership has righteousness with lawlessness? Or what fellowship has light with dark-ness?"

I had been equally yoked with Shanice, another Black girl with whom dating meant sitting together in church, holding hands, and never kissing. I had been equally yoked with Laila, who was Puerto Rican and Dominican. It meant having a crush on Tiffany and several other Black girls, not always because I liked them or because they liked me, but because we rotated within the small group of people of color. But while Raven and I were equally yoked on the surface, her sexual experience far outweighed mine.

My formal sex education began one week within a health class as a brief interruption to the regular health message of diet and exercise. Mrs. Jenkins was our health teacher, a woman in her fifties with a tiny frame, short curly hair, and big smile. She was absolutely delightful, and one of the nicest people you could meet. She also taught us the most irresponsible misinformation ever possible to keep us from having sex.

If you weren't deterred by the thought of sinning against God, fear tactics were there to help. I was taught every STD and I was made to memorize their symptoms. I learned the statistical likelihood of contracting them, but an Adventist version that took into account that we were God's chosen people, that we should know better, and that we would suffer God's wrath. "Safe" sex was a myth told by the sinful, as the only safe sex was sex you had with your husband or wife.

We were incessantly taught the importance of saving yourself for marriage, so much so that while I would fool around with Raven, I was committed to staying a virgin. Word would spread quickly if anyone was rumored to be having sex, and besides being the subject of Christian gossip, the worst kind of gossip, the students who were having sex also had to worry about expulsion if the administration found out.

Since students were assumed to be abstinent, condoms weren't available. They were contraband like meat or caffeinated drinks, but even more dangerous, because having condoms implied that you were sexually active, and being sexually active could get you expelled. Having condoms was riskier than not having them.

Despite GLAA's rules, though, faculty couldn't be everywhere to enforce them, and they knew we were ninjas with subterfuge even if they couldn't always prove it. That's where sex education week intervened. Are you okay with hurting Jesus? Are you willing to risk pregnancy? Would you like a disease?

There was a lot of false science about condoms, I was told. Mrs. Jenkins once explained AIDS in a metaphor by describing the virus as the size of a baseball, compared to the microscopic spaces in condoms that were like a volleyball net. Even if I wore a condom, it wouldn't do anything. The virus could easily go straight through, like throwing a baseball at that volleyball net.

Abstinence-only sex education succeeded in making me afraid of sex, while at the same time I was obsessed with it. I continued my tightrope walk between fear and desire, experimenting with sexual activity while doing my best to not actually *have* sex.

One day, when the bell rang after Mrs. Jenkins' class about the HIV virus soaring through the net of a condom, Raven led me to a secret bathroom backstage of the school auditorium. The auditorium was empty and locked, but we managed to get inside. We could have hidden there for hours if we wanted, and places like these marked our sexual milestones like making out in stairwells, fingering under dresses in the church pews, blowjobs in the back seat of home-leave buses while her best friend sat beside us to throw off our chaperones.

I sat on the bathroom toilet as she straddled me and reveled in the thrill of what we were doing, but also that she wanted me at all. The thrill tipped into fear, though, when she reached down to put me inside of her. We had done this dance before. I would splash in the pool but not dive in, still feeling safe enough to call myself a virgin, but Raven wasn't a virgin, and she wanted to have sex even after Mrs. Jenkins' classes about why we shouldn't. *Especially* after Mrs. Jenkins' classes on why we shouldn't. Where I was terrified, Raven was determined in her own personal resistance to what we were being taught. She would look at the contradictions of Adventist sexuality and navigate them on her own terms, with her own choices.

Our dance continued this time as it had in other bathrooms and on field trips, where she would try to put me inside of her and I would panic, telling her we had to stop. One time she managed to put me partway inside of her, which I later told Alex Mason about. Alex took to calling me a "virg" from then on because I'd lost half the word. But Raven got upset this time, gave me a shove and fixed her clothes, annoyed with who she was dealing with, a person who would break the rules, sneak through the admin building, and round third base, but found it pious to stop when he was partway inside her. And I felt bad, not because I lost her, but because I started to think she was right.

But masturbation wasn't a safe option, either. We were taught that masturbation was harmful and sinful, with at least one dorm worship every few months dedicated to the importance of avoiding it. Yet living in a building of 100 teenage boys meant it was essentially a semen factory, so much so that if you turned on a black light in any given room it would look like an indoor paintball arena. That didn't stop pastors and specialists from coming to our chapels and encouraging us against self-abuse and sins of the flesh. We were given strategies to resist our desires, like staying hydrated, physical exercise, and raising our arms above our heads. I can't recall the scientific rationale for raising our arms, but it was meant to help.

Asking forgiveness after sexual activity became the new cursing, happening every time at first, then every Sabbath to account for the week, then every few months during an altar call. Until eventually I stopped asking.

One day, I was chosen to help Dean Holt send a message to our student body about sex. He asked me if I would be willing to help, and I said yes, so the next morning at chapel Dean Holt stood in front of the student body with a flat, square box on the floor beside him and asked me to come to the stage. He handed me a box of pizza and spoke into the microphone as he gave me my instructions. I was to choose anyone in the audience I wanted to give a slice to.

I followed his directions, walking up and down the aisles, giving away a slice of pizza that had been delivered the day before, but was now rubbery and cold. I chose one friend, then two, then three. I kept going until he eventually called me back to the stage and shared his last set of instructions.

"Imagine someone special," he told me. "The most perfect girl you could think of."

He invited a girl from the audience to represent that person, another participant he had chosen to play a part.

"Now ask him," he told her.

She played her part, and asked me for a slice of pizza, but when I opened the box there was nothing left.

"Being intimate with someone…it's like this pizza," he said. "You give parts of yourself each time. And if you give all your pizza away, you won't have any left for the special person God has planned for you. Your husband or your wife. If you give it all away, there won't be anything left."

What a crock of shit, I thought.

I didn't apologize for the swearing. Or the thought.

CHAPTER 21

FINDING MISS GROTKE

My senior year at GLAA saw me in a Sophomore English class. It was the last class I needed to replace the credits I had lost, and passing it would mean I had successfully completed my last two years of high school within a year and a half. But I wasn't worried about whether I would pass. I had been on an academic tear, making up for lost time and hoping to raise my GPA enough for a goal I had only just set for myself. I wanted to go to a non-Adventist college.

The decision came as result of my relationships with David Fayed and Carlos Garcia, who would become two of my closest friends. David's family lived in Kalamazoo, Michigan, a college town that held Western Michigan University where he planned to attend. Jordan Marshall was one of the only people I knew who had openly planned not to attend college, and David was one of the only people I knew who was openly planning to leave the Adventist school system for a public university. That wasn't how it was supposed to work in the Seventh-day Adventist school pipeline, where you would go from a place like Metro to a place like GLAA to a place like

Andrews University, or Southern University, or Loma Linda.

But Darryl had recently attended Andrews University and was dropping out. It had been his first experience in the Seventh-day Adventist school system, and he hated it. *I* was used to the Adventist rules that regulated what you did and where you could go and what you could eat and what you could do on the Sabbath. Darryl was not. He found himself there partly from religious conviction, as he was going through his own journey with loving and leaving the Seventh-day Adventist church, but also because it was easy to get in. He had been thinking of college during his senior year at Detroit Urban high school, but he had not actually applied anywhere, and most college application deadlines had passed. Enrolling in Andrews though had ultimately been as easy as applying a week before, and then showing up on campus in the Adventist Mecca of Berrien Springs, Michigan. Not only did he struggle from the unfamiliar lack of freedom, but Andrews was expensive as well. At $25,000 a year, it would have costed him over $100,000 to graduate with a degree, so he would cut his losses and leave.

David wanted me to join him at Western Michigan, which I told him I would think about, but I couldn't see it happening. I had never even *been* to Kalamazoo. I had spent years moving between Metro, Oakwood, and GLAA. I was a product of the Seventh-day Adventist school system. I was scared of attending a public school. Attending Andrews would be the path of least resistance. Andrews was the next step in the pipeline.

But between Darryl leaving Andrews and David pressuring me every chance he got, I finally decided to apply to Western Michigan University. The door was there, if only I was brave enough to walk through it.

The rest of the year was spent taking school more seriously than I ever had. I studied with Carlos in the classes we had together, memorizing all 43 presidents and their political parties and flipping through flash cards with the details of Watergate. When we had the opportunity for extra credit in Advanced Literature, we took it by reciting Robert Frost's "Stopping by Woods on a Snowy Evening." We drilled each other over and over, one person quoting each line while the other echoed it.

"Whose woods these are I think I know."

"Whose woods these are I think I know."

"His house is in the village though."

"His house is in the village though."

"He will not see me stopping here."

"He will not see me stopping here."

"To watch his woods fill up with snow."

"To watch his woods fill up with snow."

"Faster!"

"Whose woods these are I think I know."

We recited that poem until we could recite it in our sleep. We'd become a clique, Carlos, David, and I, along with a few other friends, mostly the other people of color in our senior class. We sat at the Black table in the center of the cafeteria, and as the year passed it turned into our own United Nations of Black and Puerto Rican and Egyptian and Mexican and Dominican students. Even Mark, the white kid from Metro who once told me "rap" was one letter short of "crap" and "rape," found himself talking about Talib Kweli's new song "Get By" with Carlos and me. Mark was the token white person in our group. As I looked around that table at my new friends, I was reminded of one of the best cartoons to ever take a rag-tag group of kids and watch them learn to navigate as they found their way into trouble and worked their way out. I felt like I was at *Recess*.

TJ Detweiler, Vince LaSalle, Ashley Spinelli, Gretchen Grundler, Mikey Blumberg, and Gus Griswald were the best clique ever assembled. Gretchen was the tall, skinny genius who was the smarts of the squad. Spinelli was the tomboy spitfire who stood up to anybody. Mikey was the gentle giant, Vince was the moral compass, TJ was the leader, and Gus was the new character through whom we could all learn about the playground world and all its rules. None of that seemed original, yet *Recess* did what most cartoons struggled to get right, present a range of characters with enough depth that their clichés no longer mattered.

By focusing on character development and our attachment to them as individuals, *Recess* trusted its audience to look past the surface to recognize their distinctness, even as the show fell into the standard racial five-to-one ratio. Much of that could be attributed to Vince LaSalle, who was the standard token Black athlete on the surface but was a dynamic kid underneath it. Vince was Black and played basketball, but he was also kind and calm, and his integrity was what grounded the group as good kids wanting to do right as they unknowingly learned about life. I loved that he played basketball because that wasn't all he was, and I played basketball too, and as far as I was concerned, he was the glue that made every one of his friends better. Without Vince LaSalle, TJ Detweiler was just Dennis the Menace.

Aside from its main characters, my favorite aspect of the series was the world it built in the small space of a simple playground. It had rules, hierarchies, and cultures through which we suspended our belief, accepted the laws of the playground, and watched our characters as they navigated them. *Recess* built a world the size of Hogwarts with a fraction of the space. My favorite example was when the badass of the squad, known only by her last name, Spinelli, had her first name revealed to be Ashley. Spinelli was the tough kid at recess, but the rules of the playground said that anyone named Ashley had to join "the Ashleys," so off Spinelli went to join the gossipy mean girls. From the laws of becoming an Ashley, to the importance of battle tag, to Gus having to be called "the new kid" until a new "new kid" arrived, the playground in *Recess* had as many ridiculous and perplexing rules as the campus where I sat in that cafeteria at GLAA.

In *Recess*, there was the oppressive Ms. Finster, like so many of GLAA's faculty who enforced its rules. There was Randall Weems, the class snitch, the same kind of white kid who thrived at GLAA, who loved it, who would put their kids through the same punishment if they had the chance. But there was also Ms. Grotke, the teacher who found joy and wanted to spread it as best she could.

A Black woman full of optimism for her students, Ms. Grotke's joy was contagious, even when it wasn't understood. She was weird, and she shared her eccentricities as a gift to her students because she actually loved them. She wanted them to learn, not to just follow a curriculum or be scared into compliance, but to actually *learn*. She assigned her classroom to analyze how a male-written Constitution helped shape our gender-discriminating society. She discussed Beowulf as a metaphor for man's cruelty towards endangered species. Ms. Grotke dropped bars that could get her fired.

"And so, the noble Native Americans shared their bountiful food supplies with the undeserving European savages," she said to her class, one of the brief insights into her lectures before the bell rang and recess began.

Happy, hippie, and hopelessly optimistic, Ms. Grotke was the teacher I wanted. And although there wasn't a single Black teacher at GLAA, there was an eccentric white one who loved what she taught, and whose voice would get high pitched when she got excited, and who cared enough to offer me extra credit when I needed it by memorizing poems and reciting them. Her name was Ms. Waters.

Ms. Waters was the type of teacher who made a fool of herself for education. She was also the type of teacher that kids gossiped about, a single mom who was rumored to have had a divorce, making her the target of Adventist teen rumors about what happened to her marriage and how she was raising her Elementary school-aged son. Students who made fun of her only made me like her more. She seemed to *know* they were making fun of her, but she didn't care. At least, she didn't care enough to stop making a fool of herself as she tried her best to get us to care about what she was teaching.

I was hardly her star student, but I quietly admired her as she would crescendo her voice in a dramatic reading or flail her arms to make a point. My favorite class of hers, Speech and Writing, had us standing onstage where she would teach specific lessons on methods of public speaking, and then she would always go first to try to show us how it was done, being vulnerable in front of a group of teens as she spoke uninterrupted for five minutes and tried to practice the lesson she had just preached. Sometimes she was great, and other times she failed, and it was the failures that endeared her to me. She wasn't the perfect teacher, but she was a teacher who tried, and whether she succeeded or failed, she tried to laugh. She rounded out my experience at GLAA with the something I had been looking for, an adult to look up to. She never preached to me or assigned hours, in fact she hardly seemed aware of GLAA's rules at all. She just wanted me to love reading, to love writing, to love speaking, and if making a fool of herself was the price of doing it, it was one she was willing to pay. And she couldn't have known for sure, but it was working.

Back at the cafeteria at GLAA, I sat with my friends as we planned for graduation. I was on my way out of the school system I was made to join five years earlier. I had lost Jason, and Allen, and Xavier, and Terrell, and I wouldn't speak to them again. Austin Wilson would stay an open racist who would graduate with honors, but everyone would ignore the racist part. Kyle would stay white.

Cliff was gone.

But I had Jordan, who would forego college to start his career in construction and pay for my meals when I was broke in college. I had David, who would pick me up from my college dorm room and drive me to class. I had Carlos, who would tell me how capable I was, and that the only hope some people had was that I might not know it.

I had my grandma, aunt, uncle, and cousins who would come from North Carolina to watch me graduate, to yell "Represent" and retell stories of how the city boys represented.

I had my dad who was back in the picture, and who would try to make up for lost time.

I had my mom, who despite her struggles, did the best she could to love me. To take care of me. To protect me from the dangers she saw until I could learn to protect myself.

And I had Darryl. Darryl, who would drive for four hours to surprise me at boarding school and watch me play basketball. Darryl, who would be at my high school graduation, who would be at my college graduation, and who would fly to Japan to visit me. Darryl was my Optimus Prime, my

Bruce Lee, my Goliath, my Moses, my Vegeta, and my Azeem all rolled in one. My brother who was always there, who would always love me as a whole person.

I was special to him, but that wouldn't be enough.

I would learn to be special enough for myself, too.

AFTERWORD

My earliest memories reach back to 17164 Braille, the house where Darryl and I lived with both our parents, but I don't have a mental image of all of us in the same room. I remember being in the kitchen with my dad, but mom must've been in another room. I remember being in my room with my mom, but dad must've been out at work. An image of their marriage evades sight like a speck in my eye that keeps one step ahead my vision, always to the peripheral. We never had the TV family I wanted. We never sat around a table to have dinner. Dinner was a meal made by yourself with whatever you could find in the refrigerator and combine onto a plate, meant to be eaten side by side with a sibling in bed or on the couch as you watched TV and stole from the plate of whoever combined their findings better.

It was like that with my college roommates. I graduated from Great Lakes Adventist Academy in 2003 with a graduating class of about 50 students. They were destined for Andrews University or Southern University in Tennessee, but I would choose another path to attend Western Michigan University. There I shared a roommate-sibling relationship with one of my college roommates, David, where our dinner routine consisted of evenings on the couch watching our favorite hour-long drama, plates in our laps and TV straight ahead. We were both poor and ate pasta nearly every day, often straight from the pot we cooked it in. We would time it perfectly so that our food would be ready when the show began. We couldn't eat without TV, and we couldn't watch TV without eating.

For me, our evenings felt like finding comfort in the familiar and sharing it with someone who seemed to have had a similar family culture as I had had, one where you would mostly fend for yourself, along with a brother or friend. We sat watching HBO's *The Wire* or FX's *The Shield*, sharing an unspoken validation that neither of us had the "normal" family, and for us this was the normal we came to love. David's parents had recently divorced, and my mom had divorced from Cliff, and I was free to make my own feeling of home.

When high school turned to college, my exposure to the wider world began to make reciting the fourth commandment in unison with one hundred other people seem less a point of pride. Looking back on my experiences, the gradual, emotional devastation that comes from being raised with a pious upbringing and walking away from it slowly, deliberately teaching myself and unlearning things I had always thought to be true, felt like the loneliest feeling in the world. Many of those beliefs defined who I was and abandoning them meant having to rebuild myself into the person I would want to be.

I tried to change my family at times, like when I cooked that family dinner, to turn us into what I thought was a more normal one. I wanted the picture of the ideal family, the one I thought everyone else had. But we weren't the Huxtables with their obstetrician father, lawyer mother, and five kids, the picture of a perfect Black home. We weren't anything like what I saw on TV or in movies. But I knew how to cherry pick what I needed from what I saw, finding lessons in everything from *The Proud Family* to Piccolo. When I left for college, it was *A Different World*.

A spin-off from *The Cosby Show*, *A Different World* was meant to feature the Huxtable's oldest daughter, Denise, as she found herself going through college at a fictional historically Black college called Hillman. And it did, at least for a TV moment, until Lisa Bonet, the actress portraying Denise, became pregnant in real life and ultimately left the show. That unforeseen change was a blessing in disguise, though, as it left space for other characters to flourish. In season two, *A Different World* found its full potential as a show that highlighted some of the best in Black students and families, while addressing issues *The Cosby Show* wouldn't face as directly, like affirmative action, HIV, police brutality, racism, classism, and interracial relationships.

What *A Different World* became was a stark divergence from its original conception. *A Different World* was initially planned from a White perspective to follow a young Meg Ryan, a white girl in a Black school, an experience to which white viewers could relate as she navigated the social world of Black folk in a sort of voyeuristic approach to cultural awareness. Instead, we were blessed with Jeleesa, Freddie, Ron, Kim, Whitley, and Dwayne Cleophus Wayne, an iconic group of Black students who showed us countless dynamics of coming of age in Black America.

"I know my parents love me," I would scream the opening words of the theme song, watching old episodes after being reunited with TV in college. "Stand behind me come what may."

Its theme song epitomized what I wanted in terms of faith in myself and support from others. It evoked thoughts of mentors who, whether by blood or community ties or by the Blackness of our skin and the shared experience that comes with it, would take a vested interest in my potential. They would think I was special and would want me to make it. They would tell me that I was in a whole new ballgame now, with no more Cliff or GLAA, no forced church attendance, no imposed beliefs but the ones I wanted. They would tell me that while it might feel like it was me against the world, that I'd never be alone because they would be cheering for me.

The desire to make them proud, the subtle fear of letting them down, and the lingering desire to prove white people wrong, all contributed to my searching for self-worth in personal accomplishments in my years after Cliff, Metro, and GLAA. The feeling I got from working hard during my senior year of high school to catch up on credits, and the reactions I got from people who saw my hard work, replaced the sense of worth I previously felt in just being a "good Christian." I triple-majored in college. I minored in Japanese. I worked night shifts in the computer lab. I took 22 credits in one semester. I would graduate from college, join the Peace Corps, pass the Foreign Service exam, go to graduate school, and chase and chase and chase for all those accomplishments to show I was worth something.

The writer William Evans once called watching *A Different World* "praying at the altar of Black excellence," and that's exactly what it felt like. And before each sermon, before the pastor took stage, the guitar strummed that familiar opening riff, and the choir rang with "I know my parents love me." And the congregation sang. And the church said "Amen." I found motivation in Jaleesa's exams and Xavier's activism and Dwayne's aspirations. I used them to fuel my accomplishments, and while I'm grateful for my opportunities and accomplishments, I wish I had understood sooner that I was worth something even without them.

Later, I began to re-watch TV shows and movies from my childhood. I had the emotional distance to reconsider them with a more mature mind and put them in the context of where I had been in my life when I watched them. I developed an appreciation for the talented people of color who had voiced life into some of my favorite characters, who had helped me through my journey of childhood and adolescence. With characters of color already underrepresented in animation, these artists were behind the scenes all along, winning my love through their voices without me knowing who they were.

Dave Fennoy was a king of voice acting, voicing nearly one hundred characters from Nick Fury on *Ultimate Spider-Man* to Lee Everett, Warpath, or Pong Krell.

Arthur Burghardt was an early trailblazer for Black voice actors who played villains in some of my favorite television cartoons. I knew him as Destro, Devestator, and as Goofy's bully, Pete.

Brock Peters was best known for his role as Tom Robinson in *To Kill a Mockingbird*, but he also voiced roles in *Batman: The Animated Series*, *SWAT Kats*, *Captain Planet*, *Aaahh!!! Real Monsters*, and *Samurai Jack*, from which I knew him as Dark Kat, Lucius Fox, and Soul Power.

Cree Summer was the eccentric hippie-turned-lawyer in *A Different World* but was also one of the most sought-after voice talents on television. From *Tiny Toons* and *Rugrats* to the DC and Marvel Universes, her voice will forever be part of my childhood as Penny, Elmyra, and Hyena.

The beloved James Avery will always be remembered as Uncle Phil, but I'll also remember him as Shredder in *Teenage Mutant Ninja Turtles*, a role he mastered from 1987 to 1993. *The Fresh Prince of Bel-Air*, in which he played Uncle Phil, made its debut in 1990, so for three years he simultaneously held down two of the most recognizable pop culture figures of a decade. Kevin Michael Richardson would also voice Shredder, along with Bulkhead and Martian Manhunter.

Best known as Cliff Huxtable's father on *The Cosby Show*, Earle Hyman was also Panthro in *ThunderCats*.

MADtv alum Phil LaMarr was Green Lantern, Hermes Conrad, Samurai Jack, and Static.

LeVar Burton was Kwame, the first of Captain Planet's Planeteers to discover his ring and manipulate his element, Earth.

Jaleel White was Steve Urkel, but he was also Sonic the Hedgehog in both hit cartoons *Sonic the Hedgehog* and *Sonic Underground*.

Dorian Harewood was part of nearly everything I ever loved, and voiced War Machine, Martian Manhunter, and Modo from *Biker Mice from Mars*.

And then there was *Gargoyles*, my favorite cartoon of all time. Keith David voiced Goliath and Salli Richardson-Whitfield played Elisa Maza, and they were the best Black television relationship I ever knew. The list goes on and on. I found joy in recognizing and revisiting the Black-coded characters I loved, many voiced by Black actors, many of them not.

I would re-watch *A Goofy Movie* and rediscover it as a Black nerd classic. In the wake of *A Different World* ending, in came an unlikely hero I had never heard of as a child, and his name was Maximilian "Max" Goof, voiced by Jason Marsden. Max was the quintessential misunderstood high schooler, representing the need I felt through those years to have a family to be proud of, and to find my place to fit in.

There wasn't a direct villain, like there was in most Disney movies. There was Pete, but he was less a villain and more of an antagonist to go around, not go through. Instead, *A Goofy Movie* was about learning to be proud of yourself, your family, and what you had.

I could relate. It was a long journey before I would feel comfortable discussing the circumstances that made me who I am, a time when I was too embarrassed of what others would think.

Despite being a good kid, Max also had a bad persona. He was misunderstood by Principal Mazur, who recklessly labeled him based solely on his baggy clothes. Granted, Max did once highjack a school assembly, and I never did anything like that, but the principal was eager to brand him.

"Dressed like a gang member," he told Goofy, "your son caused the entire student body to break out in a riotous frenzy. If I were you, Mr. Goof, I'd seriously reevaluate the way you're raising your child before he ends up in the electric chair."

Max did reach his hood pinnacle at Lester's Possum Park, though, when he smacked the shit out a mascot that tried to hug him.

A Goofy Movie came with one last surprise for Black kids like me, and that was Tevin Campbell. Tevin "Can We Talk?" Campbell. Tevin "I'm Ready" Campbell. Being cast as Powerline, one of the most popular R&B singers of my childhood was placed front and center of its fictional universe, calling him "the greatest rock star in the world." Our Tevin Campbell. Our vest-wearing, S-curl styling, soul singing Tevin Campbell.

"Stand out above the crowd, even if I gotta shout out

loud. Till mine is the only face you'll see, gonna stand out till you notice me." I felt like it was written specifically for me.

And the dance choreography? Not limited to Powerline, the whole troop had fire. Max saved Goofy's life in the Perfect Cast scene and turned it into the street's hottest dance. Goofy made it a hot line, Max made it a hot song. Goofy dropped, twirled, jumped, put his hands on his hips and fucking moon-walked. Powerline looked at him like "who is this n…oh my god, I'll allow it."

I'd go to a party and drop those moves right now. Max killed the game, and Roxanne and her home girl saw it and started doing it on the spot. It was a dream.

And in the midst of it all was the movie's climax. Not kissing Roxanne, not hugging his dad. The most triumphant moment of *A Goofy Movie* was when Max made it onstage, and his homies saw him. The exact moment Pauly Shore screams, "That's Max! Max is on the tuu-uuuube! That's Max, I know him!" It makes me cry every time. Nothing compares to "Max is on the tuu-uuuube! That's Max, I know him!"

He did it, y'all. That single moment summarized every-thing Max ever wanted. Validation. For people to be proud of him the way he was never proud of his dad. For someone to claim him. To be special. To be loved. He did it, and I saw him do it. Do you have any idea how powerful that was to 10-year-old me? It stands eternal in my heart. *A Goofy Movie* remains the Blackest, most underrated nerd classic of all time for the message it sent to a young Black kid who wanted to fit in. Whose affirmations were so subtle that they'd instill a seed of confidence that we never actually saw planted.

"That's Max. Max is on the tube. I know him."

I do too, Pauly Shore. I do, too.

ACKNOWLEDGMENTS

I'm eternally grateful for friends and strangers who nudged me along, people who helped make this book happen without knowing it.

There were many who played a role, from Ben Taylor at Lit Riot Press who pushed me to turn it from a series of essays into the memoir it became, to friends from the dog park who asked how it's coming along, to strangers on social media who sent an encouraging Instagram message or enthusiastic tweet.

In between are many of the most important people in my life. It goes without saying that there are too many to name here, and that "thank you" is hardly enough to convey how grateful I am or begin to tell you what you mean to me.

To Daryn Cohen, Sara Ray, Omar Holmon, Natasha Singh-Holmon, William Evans, Alessandro Allegranzi, Samer and Aysu Saliba, CB Rucker, Natalie Relich, Kiley Ong, Tina Park, Shanelle Little, Ali Robbins, Gabe Montes, everyone at *Black Nerd Problems*, and the best book club that ever existed, thank you for being who you are.

To mom, dad, my nephews Darryl and Desmond, my sister-in-law Stefanie, and my brother Darryl, thanks for being my family.

ABOUT THE AUTHOR

Jordan Calhoun is a culture writer living in New York City. He is the Editor-in-Chief at *Lifehacker*, publishes a weekly newsletter about ethics and culture on *The Atlantic* called Humans Being, and he is a regular contributor as a culture writer for *Black Nerd Problems*. Calhoun is a returned Peace Corps Volunteer, he holds a B.A. in Sociology and Criminal Justice, a B.S. in Psychology from Western Michigan University, and an M.P.A. in Public Policy from New York University. Calhoun's writing appears in *The Atlantic*, *Black Nerd Problems*, *Huffington Post*, *Vulture*, and more. *Piccolo Is Black: A Memoir of Race, Religion, and Pop Culture* is his debut memoir.

CPSIA information can be obtained
at www.ICGtesting.com
Printed in the USA
BVHW032047170422
634551BV00005B/141

9 781735 145815